D0922130

The**Pax**Story

ThePaxStory

Service in the Name of Christ
1951-1976

Calvin W. Redekop

Foreword by Ronald J. R. Mathies

Pandora Press U.S.
Telford, Pennsylvania

copublished with
Herald Press
Scottdale, Pennsylvania

Pandora Press U.S. orders, information, reprint permissions:
pandoraus@netreach.net
1-215-723-9125
126 Klingerman Road, Telford PA 18969
www.PandoraPressUS.com

The Pax Story
Copyright © 2001 by Pandora Press U.S., Telford, PA 18969
All rights reserved
Copublished with Herald Press, Scottdale, PA
Library of Congress Catalog Number: 2001034638
ISBN: 0-1-931038-00-7
Printed in Newton, Kansas by Mennonite Press
Book design by Pandora Press U.S.
Cover design by Gwen M. Stamm

The paper used in this publication is recycled and meets the
minimum requirements of American National Standard for Information Sciences—Permanence of Paper for Printed Library Materials,
ANSI Z39.48-1984.1984

All Bible quotations are used by permission, all rights reserved, and
are from the *New Revised Standard Version Bible*, copyright 1989, by the
Division of Christian Education of the National Council of the
Churches of Christ in the USA.

Library of Congress Cataloguing-in-Publication Data
Redekop, Calvin Wall, 1925-
    The Pax story: service in the name of Christ, 1951-1976 / Calvin W.
Redekop ; foreword by Ron Mathies
        p. cm.
    Includes bibliographical references (p.) and index.
    ISBN 1-931038-00-7
    1. Pax (Organization)--History. 2. Conscientious objectors--United
States--History--20th century. 3. Mennonites--United States--
Charities--History--20th century. I. Title

    BX8128.W4 R43 2001
    267'.1897--dc21

                                                                  2001034638

10 09 08 07 06 05 04 03 02 01   10 9 8 7 6 5 4 3 2 1

Dedicated to the roughly 1,150 U.S. and Canadian young men who by faith obeyed the call and left kindred and home, not knowing where they were to go (or what they were to do), but looked forward to the city, with firm foundation, whose architect and builder is God.

Contents

Foreword

Christ taught love and that is what his children must do. These words of Pax volunteer Daniel Gerber, who served and disappeared in Vietnam in the early 1960s, summarize the motivation for the story contained in these pages. This volume is being released on the fiftieth anniversary of the founding of the Pax program. Over two decades Pax sent more than a thousand volunteers to over thirty countries to alleviate human need and build bridges of understanding and peace.

How does one evaluate the work of a program such as Pax? Does one measure the work accomplished through the number of houses, other structures, and highways constructed? The number of refugees fed and resettled? The amount of relief and agricultural rehabilitation completed? The quantity of peace camps conducted? Does one try to measure the impact on the individuals and organizations assisted?

Certainly the impact on the Mennonite Central Committee has been profound. The Pax program led the way for people to become the most important part of MCC service. The word *Pax* became the symbol for service and peace for a whole generation. The linkage of relief, reconstruction, rehabilitation with peace predated and shaped the later concepts of development and accompaniment. Indeed, Pax was part of the glue that helped form a sense of the global church community.

Not least, however, was the impact on the volunteers themselves. One need but listen to their stories, note the glistening eyes, or hear the catch in their voices to understand that their assignments were indeed the most significant experiences in their lives. Those years away from home led to life-long relationships and new educational, vocational, and avocational directions on their return. New global worldviews were forged. Service "in the name of Christ" became at once a most fruitful bond and motivation.

A recent book on the Mennonite contribution to international peacebuilding suggests that it is the quiet, gentle, respectful, and noncompetitive manner of being with those struggling with life's deepest challenges and darkest tragedies that allows people to discover a constructive and courageous way forward. Surely the participants of the Pax program helped to shape that understanding of service.

—*Ronald J. R. Mathies*
   Executive Director, Mennonite Central Committee

Author's Preface

Gloria in excelsis Deo, et in terra pax[1]

After a rough crossing over the Atlantic on the small Dutch Leerdam, twenty young American farm boys arrived on the shores of Europe on April 6, 1951.[2] This was barely six years after the end of World War II which had severely damaged Belgium, France, Italy, the Netherlands, and especially Germany. The boys docked at Antwerp, which before the war had been one of the most picturesque harbors of Europe.

Peter Neufeld, a Paxer, noted, "We went through customs when they opened at 9:20. There to meet us were Cal Redekop and Paul Ruth with a fancy Dutch Bus."[3] The bus began to worm its way along winding paths through huge mounds of rubble of what had been the busy and beautiful city, and headed for Espelkamp.

Neufeld continues, "We arrived at Espelkamp at 8:45 p.m., got stuck in mud and had to get out and push the big bus out. The first night we had to sleep in an ammunition bunker without any heat."[4] This description of their arrival at the wharf and their primitive accommodations, illustrates that these young men had come to help to rebuild war-torn Europe.[5]

For the men and women who participated in it, the Pax story is one of the most significant experiences of their lives. When Pax is discussed, Pax men almost always say, "The Pax experience was the turning point of my life," or "the Pax years were the most important years of my life." But those not familiar with it may well ask, "What is Pax?" Or "Why should I know about Pax?" Ironically those of us who were in it, often have a difficult time explaining its nature and its importance, at least to us. Pax was so unusual, so personal, and so powerfully meaningful, that it is hard to put the experience into words.

Similarly, it is practically impossible to write a history of Pax because Pax was so varied. Each person's perspective on Pax is different—the perspective of the first Pax men who helped build homes for German refugees in the early 1950s differs dramatically from the experiences of the men who served in Afghanistan, India, the Dominican Republic and Haiti, and Vietnam in the 1960s and 1970s (some of the last countries to receive Pax service).

In between these periods there were men who worked in a vast variety of places. In the Congo, for example, Pax men underwent experiences that ran the gamut from eating grasshoppers to nearly being killed by insurgents. In Bolivia, Paxers helped move Quechua Indians from the Alto Plano to the eastern jungle.[6]

It is impossible to include every Pax man's unique work and experiences in *The Pax Story.* A full history would have to include the experiences of each Pax fellow, of Pax men in specific units, a description of all the projects and what they accomplished, the names of all the Pax men, the unit leaders, the matrons, Pax pastors and the like. An overview of Pax can only be presented by generalizing and glossing over many differences and details.

So this book is not *the* history of Pax. Rather it is a brief, basic review of the various factors contributing to the origins of the Pax idea and a survey of how the Pax idea was realized through some 1,200 volunteers participating in projects in more than forty countries around the globe. It is also a discussion of the significance of a quarter century of extraordinary service, (1951-1976) and for the later history of volunteerism and efforts to bring peace to the world—in *terra pax.*

Hopefully this Pax history will provide the context and framework into which each Pax person can insert his or her own experience to round out and complete the picture. Others who were not privileged to participate in Pax directly may also want to know the story and evaluate its validity. Finally, this story is offered to the general reader with the conviction that it has a moral for the citizens of the world.

No Pax volunteer will deny that Pax was an exciting and noble phenomenon. Peter J. Dyck, long-time worker in Europe both during and after World War II, has said, "I have also experienced war, notably in England when the German Luftwaffe bombed the British cities. In Manchester, England, I twice faced the judge for refusing to serve in the military. If I were a young American of draft age today, I would go the way of Pax."[7]

The challenging and heart warming story in these pages will lead most readers to reflect on the following questions: What were the consequences of the Pax idea for the participants and for the recipients? And for the rest of us, what impact did it have for the larger world? Additionally, what are the equivalent challenging needs and opportunities for the idealists of our day, whether young or old? Why did the idea end, or did it serve out its useful life? What are the functional equivalents for a Pax effort working for reconciliation and peace in our day, or will we need to continue to rebuild what future wars will destroy?

—*Calvin W. Redekop*
  Harrisonburg, Virginia

Acknowledgments

Pax men cherish the Anabaptist faith tradition that nurtured them to believe that it is better to give than to receive, and that the greatest of all commandments is to love one another. So we thank God for our spiritual forebears.

Further we especially acknowledge the gift of the Mennonite Central Committee (MCC), which is also a product of the Anabaptist heritage. No Paxer will ever be able to fully describe what MCC has meant and what it has done. So we thank MCC for what it has done for us, including presenting an expanded world and its opportunities to us in ways we would never have dreamed.

We give profound thanks to our congregations, parents, and families who supported us while we went overseas to serve "in the name of Christ."

Finally, as author I thank the members of the planning committee for Pax 50, the September 2001 fifty-year Pax celebration/reunion, which strongly supported the idea of producing the story of Pax. They are Bruce Aurenheimer, Robert Ediger, Owen Hess, John Hiebert, James Juhnke, Arlo Kasper, Al Keim, Bill Klassen, Orville Schmidt, Robert Schrag, Walter Schmucker, George Steckly, Mark Wadel, and Dwight Wiebe (who did not live to enjoy the fifty-year celebration/reunion on September 14-16, 2001).

The destruction of the center of Frankfurt/Main, taken from the church tower facing east in 1950. Calvin W. Redekop photo.

Menno Gaeddert guiding the first Pax group around the same church facing west. Calvin W. Redekop photo.

Introduction: The Pax Program in Perspective

Helping history become more just, free, equal, and nonviolent is the heart of the pacifist enterprise. In the twentieth century binding up the wounds inflicted by the violent history-makers has been a particular vocation of those most persistent pacifists, the historic peace churches (the Mennonites, the Church of the Brethren, and the Friends). They have constituted a tiny assemblage—some hundreds of thousands of souls—united in their refusal to join the crusades to make history come out right.

An obvious example from the Cold War era is their refusal to join the effort to create either a Pax Americana, or a Pax Sovietica. That pacifist refusal, while morally and perhaps even politically defensible, did not get pacifists off the hook. Political, moral, and spiritual accountability demanded that pacifists find other ways of dealing with the tragic intractability of human history. The Pax program described in this book offers a near-perfect example of that pacifist agenda put to work.

This book describes and analyses this quintessentially Mennonite pacifist enterprise. It is an engaging and inspiring story of simple, youthful, practical Christian idealism applied to real human problems. Whether teaching Africans, Greeks, or Latin Americans new farming techniques; helping care for lepers in Vietnam; building roads in Paraguay; or building houses for refugees in Germany, the focus was always on practical solutions for the problem at hand. Pax was a program which tapped the latent talent of young men and women and gave them scope to use their ingenuity.

In 1943, Harold S. Bender had laid the groundwork for a new understanding of Anabaptism with his famous "Anabaptist Vision" essay. Twenty years later, in 1972, John Howard Yoder published his pathbreaking book, *The Politics of Jesus*, which, better than any other single work, expressed the essence of the new post-war Mennonite theology. Harold Bender made "discipleship" (*nachfolge Christi*) the centerpiece of Anabaptist-Mennonite theology. The Concern movement, which originated in Amsterdam in 1952 and included Paul Peachey, John Howard Yoder, and Calvin Redekop, embraced discipleship and added the idea of the fellowship of believers (the church) as the hermeneutical community where how to follow Jesus in life (history) became the primary focus of attention.

Discipleship became the theological justification for service, and church happened wherever "two or three gathered in his name" to find where and how to be Jesus' disciples in the world. In this new understanding the church could be a highly mobile and informal gathering of believers who went wherever their discipleship led them. With the focus on praxis, on "lived" faith, this new concept of the church was admirably suited to the needs of the burgeoning Mennonite Central Committee program in the postwar period. The Pax program fit nicely into that new understanding.

♣

Most of the men and women who served in Pax were born between 1930 and 1950, years that began and ended two of the most chaotic and violent decades in human history. In 1930 the world was in the grip of the Great Depression; in 1950 the Cold War, driven by nuclear and ideological politics, dominated human life. Bracketed in the middle—the 1940s—was World War II, a catastrophe so calamitous that it defies explanation. One can only conclude that in the birth-decades of most Pax men and women, the world suffered a global nervous breakdown.

The aftermath of World War II did not usher in a new era of peace, but brought the onset of a new form of war—the so-called "Cold War." What some at first saw as simply an aftershock of the Second World War had, by 1950, become a state of normality; a world order locked into a permanent ideological conflict between communism and democratic capitalism. Armed with atomic weaponry and deadly new delivery systems, it seemed just a matter of time before the world would again erupt into another round of world war. The formation of the People's Republic of China in 1949, and the outbreak of the Korean War in 1950 seemed to confirm those fears.

By 1950, Americans felt beleaguered. Despite their heroic efforts during the war and the expenditure of billions of dollars for postwar reconstruction, the world seemed less safe than ever before. By the late 1940s, Eastern Europe had fallen under the sway of the Soviet Union. To everyone's dismay, the Soviets quickly broke the United States' monopoly on the atomic bomb.

Many Americans suddenly found the optimistic assumption that history was on their side to be no longer credible and wanted to know why or who had "lost" the postwar peace. How could they have won the war so convincingly, only to lose the postwar peace so quickly? The result was the McCarthy era and the search for scapegoats who could be blamed for "losing the peace."

The invasion of South Korea by Communist North Korea on June 25, 1950, not only affected the destiny of millions of Asians and several hundred thousand American soldiers, but the lives of thousands of young American Mennonite conscientious objectors as well. The Korean War convinced American policymakers that the United States military must be placed on a state of permanent readiness. A key feature of such readiness was a universal conscription system to provide the necessary manpower.

Consequently, a new conscription system was put in place by the Congress just about the time the first contingent of Pax men arrived in Europe in April 1951. Over the course of the next twenty-five years, some 20,000 young Mennonites would be drafted and opt for an alternative service assignment as conscientious objectors. Of those 20,000, close to 1,200 would serve in Pax.

♣

Twentieth-century history has been brutally invasive; few people escaped some aspect of its harsh character. Mennonites in Europe and the Soviet Union felt some of history's harshest blows simply because of their physical location. Those who lived in the Western hemisphere, where the actual devastation of the two world wars was avoided, were more fortunate.

There, however, the Anabaptist faith-heritage of pacifism put Mennonites on a collision course with the public policy of their nations. As conscientious objectors in a world at war, American and Canadian Mennonites were required to test as never before, their assumptions about how to deal with the modern nation-state.

Like most of their contemporaries, Mennonites found themselves threatened, by the fury of twentieth century wars. American Mennonites first felt the effects of the Bolshevik Revolution in Russia vicariously through the starvation of thousands of Mennonites in the Ukraine, who were caught in the chaos of that great conflagration. American Mennonites responded by creating the Mennonite Central Committee (MCC) in 1920, an organization designed to feed their starving brothers and sisters. Over the course of the next eighty years, MCC became the embodiment of the Mennonite desire to cope with and remedy the cruelties visited on the weak and defenseless in the world.

World War II taught Western Mennonites that they had a special responsibility for the victims of history's calamities. World War II seemed an unusually clear example of a good war and some Mennonites felt a twinge of remorse that they could not join the crusade to rid the world of Hitler and his minions. Many Mennonites found it hard to say no to the call to arms, and more than half of all Mennonites drafted during the war endorsed the cause by joining the military.

Those who became conscientious objectors (COs) served in a special program, Civilian Public Service (CPS), operated by an unusual partnership between the historic peace churches and Selective Service. The COs worked at a variety of conservation, agricultural, and social work projects. In all, some 12,000 Mennonites, Brethren, and Quakers worked in the program during World War II.

Pax men were not only the sons of the CPS generation, but CPS became a model for the Pax program as well. Most Mennonites believed that the CPS program, with its focus on simple, hands-on service by unskilled, but capable young men, not only offered COs an alternative to war, but provided an example of how Mennonites ought to embrace post-war reconstruction.

Mennonites saw binding up the wounds of war as one way to compensate for not helping win the war. But there was another motivating discovery, within a few months of the end of the war. Western Mennonites learned that tens of thousands of Russian and Prussian Mennonites had fled west with the retreating German armies in the last months of the war, and were living under incredible hardships in refugee camps in Germany and Denmark.

The news of the plight of their sisters and brothers in the faith unleashed a flood of funds and volunteers. In response, the MCC relief program grew by leaps and bounds. So much money came in to the MCC coffers in the first years after the war that its managers were hard-put to create enough programs to deploy the new resources. Mennonites, like all American farmers, had prospered during the war, and had substantial means to fund the new relief work. By 1948, MCC had several hundred American Mennonites placed in relief and rehabilitation work in Europe.

By 1950, American Mennonites had rediscovered their European Mennonite brothers and sisters. That was a new development. During the first half of the twentieth century American Mennonites had perceived their European counterparts as fallen brethren who had lost their pacifist convictions and embraced modern liberal theology. The perception was so pervasive that only seven American Mennonites attended the 1936 Mennonite World Conference held in the Netherlands.

The 1941 *Mennonites in Europe* history by John Horsch reinforced the "fallen brethren" notion. Horsch argued that the European Mennonites had abandoned the three linchpins of early Anabaptism: nonresistance, nonconformity, and biblical literalism. The result was that the American Mennonites came out of World War II with the notion that American Mennonites were the real bearers of authentic Anabaptism.

One heartening byproduct of the massive MCC post-war relief effort was the re-connection of American and European Mennonites. The new relationships forged by the MCC relief and refugee work, which included the Pax program, led to a somewhat guileless, even smug, but nevertheless genuine American Mennonite effort to help the European Mennonites renew their Anabaptist faith heritage. Nearly 1,000 American Mennonites crossed the Atlantic to attend the 1952 Mennonite World Conference at Basel, Switzerland. Many Pax men also attended. European and American Mennonites were beginning to fellowship with each other in serious and important new ways.

By the mid-1960s, the passage of Mennonites across the Atlantic ocean had become a pilgrimage, as American Mennonites sought to rediscover and visit the scenes where early Anabaptism emerged. The American Mennonite travel organization, Tourmagination, led thousands of American Mennonites on three-week pilgrimages to visit Anabaptist and Mennonite locations and communities. The effect on Mennonite self-awareness and a sense of trans-Atlantic fellowship has been quite extraordinary.

The Pax program began with the Korean War; it ended when the Vietnam War ended. Part of the Pax élan lay in the fact that Pax men and women understood that they were saying no to the American and the world's war system. But they were also saying no to American hubris and the American way of being in the world.

In hindsight it has become apparent that the Cold War was never a true contest between two equal powers, the U.S. and U.S.S.R. The U.S. always possessed a preponderance of power, bestriding the world like a modern-day Rome and imposing its will with an intimidating array of high-tech war machinery. The trowels, paint brushes, road graders, experimental agriculture plots, pipe pumps, and more used by Pax men were an eloquent alternative to the high-tech engines of destruction brandished by the American and Soviet imperialists.

The Cold War was also an ideological contest, pitting capitalism against communism. To much of the developing world, however, it also appeared as a religious conflict, for much of American Cold War rhetoric used Christian justifications and images. The "ugly American" was also an "ugly Christian" in the eyes of many. To understand the symbolic significance of the Pax program we must see it as a way Mennonites gave life to a nonviolent way of being Christian in a world where American Christianity was perceived to be on a crusade, characterized by overwhelming power. The meek and humble work of Pax men offered a credible, and an incredible, witness to Jesus' call for another way of being in the world.

♣

No account of the Pax program should neglect the profound effect that the Pax experience had on the young men and women who served. This book offers numerous windows to that story. Many, perhaps most of the Pax men came from the farm or from blue-collar occupations although some were college educated. For most, the Pax experience was their first venture abroad and their first encounter with another language. The new sights, sounds, and smells encompassed what we now call a "cross-cultural" experience.

Educationally, we know the power of such an experience to change perceptions and to create possibilities for new behaviors. Almost without exception the Pax experience had a transformational effect on the men and women in the program. It changed their lives and often led to faith-inspired decisions regarding career directions for their lives.

But the Pax experience also had consequences for the communities to which the men returned, and the congregations where they worshiped. For twenty-five years, Pax men returned to witness to the new insights and convictions they had garnered from their time abroad. A remarkable number of the Paxers became vocationally involved in social work, education, health, and church ministry.

When one adds the many thousands of other Mennonites involved in I-W (see Appendix B for explanation of how Mennonites provided non-military service for conscientious objectors classified I-W), voluntary service, Mennonite Disaster Service, and other VS assignments the amount of activity becomes staggering. The steady year-in, year-out return of VSers to their congregations bearing stories and new knowledge has had enormous consequences for the Mennonite church.

But if Pax was so wonderful, why did it not become a bigger operation? Only about five percent of those Mennonites who were drafted during the quarter century from 1950 to 1975 chose Pax assignments. Was this a promotional failure? Was it a failure to find important projects with which to challenge young people? Did the peculiar organizational structure of the Pax program within MCC militate against innovation and new program initiatives? This book helps us think about those questions.

An equally important question is whether there are contemporary possibilities to create a Pax-like program for today's young pacifists. While there is no current military draft to generate a cadre of persons in search of alternative service assignments, we who gained so much from the Pax experience must carry some responsibility to find equivalent challenges and opportunities for our biological and spiritual grandchildren. Certainly the messy, tragic chaos of history has not lessened. The contemporary world is strewn with the victims of calamitous history. I hope this book will rekindle in all of us a renewed determination to find contemporary applications of the Pax ideals.

—*Al Keim,*
  Pax, 1955-57

ThePaxStory

International volunteers at Mainz MVS camp, building a Protestant student retreat house. Calvin W. Redekop photo

The first Mennonite Voluntary Service Board: Adriaan Swartendijk, Holland; Paul Peachey, MCC; Richard Hertzler, Germany; Andre Kauffman, France; Cal Redekop, MVS Director, H. A. Fast, MCC European Director; Sam Gerber, Switzerland. Calvin W. Redekop photo

Mennonite Voluntary Service Symbol. Calvin W. Redekop photo

Chapter 1

Forerunners
of the Pax Idea

What were the "Pax boys" thinking as they landed at the Antwerp, Belgium harbor and saw the vastness of the devastation caused by World War II?[1]

Just before leaving MCC headquarters in Akron, Pennsylvania for Europe, they had completed a fifteen-day orientation in Mennonite History and Faith, but little information was shared concerning the work in Germany. There were, however, some subtle hints in a sheet entitled BASIC CLOTHING LIST FOR MEN IN THE 1V-E BUILDERS UNIT (see Appendix A for full text). "Clothing," line 5 listed "4 pair work trousers or 4 sets combination shirts and washable pants." Line 6 stated, "1 jacket (work)" and line 17 suggests "1 pair work shoes (G.I. type)!"

There is practically no published material by former Pax men that reflects how they thought their modest efforts might diminish all that destruction. However, some of the diaries matter-of-factly describe the arrival in Europe and getting started at the work projects. Thus Peter Neufeld's diary simply states, that after a "slow trip" over the Atlantic, (from March 26 to April 6, 1951) "it was a thrill to finally see the White Cliffs of Dover on the coast of England."[2] The next entry provides a candid and laconic view of the first introduction to the vast challenge before them:

> April 11, 1951. When Cal took us to our project, I think we were a bit surprised. There were trees and stumps all over the soft wet ground. We were told that our first jobs would be to drain the area with two long ditches and then to dig

out all the stumps, build a road, dig five huge basements
and all without heavy equipment! All to be done with manpower—ours. The first few days were really rough. I believe
some of us had been expecting adventure and fun in Germany. But we were quickly reminded that we actually had
volunteered to work.[3]

Those persons at the dock, or the general public that later
read about this group's arrival from America, must have been
mystified. What on earth motivated these young volunteers,
and what did they think they were going to accomplish?
Where did the idea come from? This idealistic expedition or
foolish adventure seemed to demand an explanation, but none
was immediately forthcoming. But the strangeness and au-
dacity of this venture was not missed by those who worked
closely with these "boys" on the work projects or witnessed
their activity.

The first builders unit[4] in Europe is of more than passing
interest. For this group of men was the first wave of a volunteer movement among Mennonites which would eventually
undertake reconstruction and rehabilitation of war-ravaged
communities and agricultural and community social development in socially-dislocated communities in more than forty
countries. Pax became a household word in many communities beginning in Germany and finally ending in Vietnam in
the mid-1970s. By then it included more than 1,180 volunteers
spanning twenty-five years (1951-1976).[5]

The World War I Builders Units

Where did the Pax story originate? The Pax builders units
were by no means the first Americans to volunteer to serve on
foreign soil. One of the first religious volunteer reconstruction
units to serve in Europe was organized by the American
Friends Service Committee (AFSC). Under the general direction of the American Red Cross, the AFSC sent fifty-four
Quaker men and one Mennonite to Europe on September 4,
1917, to do reconstruction work in areas of France devastated
by World War I. The volunteers understood that if any of the
men were to be drafted, they would return to stateside immediately.

In January 1918, the Mennonite Relief Committee, recently formed by the Mennonite Church, officially decided to support the AFSC project in France and began processing Mennonite young men, including a number of several conscientious objectors who had been released from prison at Fort Leavenworth, Kansas.[6] The builders units built or repaired more than 500 homes in France. The program ended in April 1, 1920, and fifty-four Mennonite men had participated. This experience was crucial for Quaker and Mennonite perspectives on world service in place of military action.

The French reconstruction effort was not forgotten by Mennonites. In 1940, the Mennonite Central Committee (MCC) began work in Lyons, France, as an extension of their children's feeding program started in 1937 in Spain.[7] This was reopened in 1945, with child feeding and clothing distribution. Then in 1946, MCC made contact with the French Mennonites and a builders unit was sent to Wissembourg to help in the reconstruction of damaged buildings including what was to become the Wissembourg children's home.[8]

In the meantime, the Mennonite Relief Committee (MRC) began relief work in Belgium in November 1945, when the MRC sent a builders unit to Belgium. The unit rebuilt a number of homes in the badly destroyed village of Bullange in eastern Belgium. The effort was intended not only to assist destitute families, but also to help with the missionary work that was just beginning in Belgium. Paul Peachy, whose role in Pax will be noted below, was part of this effort along with his wife, Ellen. The unit lasted until 1950, when David A. and Wilma Shank began missionary work in Brussels by following up on all the connections and goodwill that had been created in the region.[9]

Earlier Voluntary Service Experiments

But the idea of volunteers serving in the name of peace and reconstruction had existed already long before the Mennonites worked in Europe. Service Civil Internationale (SCI) and other international peace organizations had already been in action in Europe and other parts of the world.[10] SCI was the brain-child of Pierre Ceresole (1879-1945), the Swiss teacher, engineer, writer, lecturer, and pacifist organizer.[11] In 1917, he addressed the Fellowship of Reconciliation and urged it to put peace activism into practice. Hence "the first international alternative service program took place at Esnes near Verdun at which men from various European countries performed reconstruction work."[12] Ceresole initiated the SCI, which in turn spawned other organizations in Europe and elsewhere. The work was curtailed during World War II, but resumed immediately when the war ended.

Although volunteerism had obviously been around for a long time, it had slowly become a conscious concept. The idea of volunteering time, effort, and vision for a cause took hold and became disseminated throughout the world. This idea took many forms, including youth movements that focused on political and social ideals and goals.

Among the many ironies of the noble idea Ceresole and others dreamed up was the fact that Hitler used its framework to form the Hitler *Jugend* in Germany. The movement's goal was to create a young, nationalistic public sector that would support the goals of Nazism and supply the manpower to implement them.

To extend the German paradox even further, the significant Pax road building project in Paraguay was preceded by the creation of a youth movement called the *Jugendbund*. According to Walter Quiring, one of its founding sponsors,

> The Fernheim Jugendbund is on the march! It marches at the head of all German-Mennonite foreign colonies. In the first place, an awakened Mennonite youth is clearing away the idle notions that foreign Germans of Mennonite faith are Dutch or Mennonite Russians. We are Germans! And whoever does not like it can find other friends.[13]

The irony of this saga is that the volunteerism and service concepts promoted in these Mennonite colonies, were far removed from the goals and ideals of Ceresole and others. They also could not have been more different from Mennonite Voluntary Service which later emerged in North America and Germany after World War II, and which contributed to the Pax program, as will be shown below.

Other Recent VS Organizations and Activities

Voluntary Service emerged among Mennonites during and after World War II (see Chapter 2). One organized expression of voluntary service is Mennonite Disaster Service (MDS). The agency is a powerful illustration that volunteering for the purpose of helping others was already "in the air" by the time the Pax movement became a reality. MDS was born at Hesston, Kansas in 1950 as a response to the need to help victims of natural disasters in the United States. But its context was broader. "At the July 28, 1950, Sunday school picnic in Newton, Paul Shenk led a discussion on 'What can we as COs do to help our country and people in need now and in war?' "[14]

MDS soon evolved into a program for recruiting volunteers to move into disasters, help clean up and restore order, then rebuild homes for the flood or tornado victims, for the purpose of peace and reconciliation. The volunteers would usually stay in a community until the emergency was fully alleviated. MDS became one of the most widely known and respected movements in North American Mennonite history. There are obvious similarities in MDS and Pax which suggest that the necessary ingredients for Pax were broadly present as will be evident below. The chief differences were that Pax was international in scope and purpose, was more deeply involved in international development work than MDS, and was largely initiated and energized in response to the United States' military draft.

(above) MVS preparing the munitions bunker to be home for "Pax boys" on their arrival I Espelkamp.

(below) Pax men "digging the trenches" for the first series of refugee homes in Espelkamp. Calvin W. Redekop photos

Chapter 2

Voluntary Service and the Pax Idea

By the end of World War II voluntary service was in the bloodstream of North American Mennonites. Of the approximately 1,800 Paxmen who served between 1951 and 1976, 110 were Canadian. Lacking a draft, the Canadians must have entered the program because of their service motivation and the challenging opportunities the Pax program offered.[1]

It is interesting to note that after the program had become well-publicized, Canadian volunteers reached a high of eleven and twelve in 1960 and 1961, respectively. This indicates that congregations in both Canada and the United States had strongly nurtured the idea of service "in the name of Christ," and that the draft in the U.S. only intensified the urgency of finding outlets for service for the U.S. volunteers.

By the beginning of World War II, North American Mennonites, had been introduced to the idea of voluntary service through programs conducted by MCC and similar organizations among the Mennonite conferences. The first official voluntary service program emerged in 1943 during World War II, when Virginia Mennonites requested such an action as a response to pressure from the U.S. Civil Defense agency. Soon Mennonite conferences across the United States were actively planning voluntary service units.[2] From 1944-1946, MCC began to organize summer work camp units "in part under the influence of the Quaker summer work camps which had already begun in 1935."[3]

The Civilian Public Service program, conducted between 1941 and 1947, also played a major part in the development of the service idea and helped make Mennonites aware of the wider world. But CPS was a response to the military draft of World War II and had a rather specific set of dynamics and consequences. The drawbacks to CPS motivated church leaders to learn from the past.[4] Many of the undesirable and negative aspects of CPS were kept in mind when subsequent service programs, including Pax, were planned.

American Mennonite Students and VS

The next link in the chain leading up to the birth of Pax was European Mennonite Voluntary Service (later called MVS). Inspired in part by the voluntary service concept already existing in Europe,[5] MVS unwittingly began in fall 1946, when the Council of Mennonite and Affiliated Colleges (CMAC) initiated a program to send Mennonite young people from Europe for a summer-study program. College officials and MCC leadership gradually developed the idea that a summer in Europe, especially in Germany, would certainly broaden the educational experience of the students.[6]

The first summer exchange took place in 1947, when "a group of young people from the American Mennonite Colleges toured Western Europe and listened to lectures arranged for them at universities in Holland and Switzerland."[7] This proved less than satisfactory, since there had been little direct and intense contact with young people from Europe. The returned students' evaluations strongly indicated that there was a deep desire for more "direct contact with European Mennonite youth through the sharing of common experience." Beginning in 1948 this was remedied through short-term reconstruction and repair projects in war-devastated Germany. The projects provided intensive interaction, common work, and recreation for up to four weeks.[8]

Consequently, "through the co-operative efforts of the Council of Mennonite and Affiliated Colleges, Voluntary Service administrations [of several Mennonite groups] MCC personnel, European Mennonites, Military Government of the British and American zones, and local authorities, two units were set up" in 1948.[9] One of the two units was assigned to an old castle near Frankfurt that was being rennovated for the

Hesse Evangelical youth. The other unit helped restore a badly damaged home for epileptic and mentally handicapped people in Hamburg, also sponsored by the Evangelical Church (Lutheran).

These first work camps brought the American students in contact with a few European young people who were displaced or orphaned victims of the war looking for something meaningful. Some of these victims literally pleaded for the chance to participate in the camps, because they quickly discovered the camps were the source of a square meal. These camps, however, also provided Mennonite youth with opportunities to help local neighborhoods organize children's activities, clean up an area for a youth soccer field, help clear away rubble, or even help construct community centers, all while establishing international good will with the communities being helped.[10]

In 1949, the two camps near Frankfurt and Hamburg were followed by projects in Frankfurt, Hannover, and Stuttgart. By summer 1950, the work camps consisted of many nationalities in which American students were in the minority.[11] This led to a tradition of MCC/CMAC sponsored summer work camps for select American Mennonite college students. The camps were located in heavily war-devastated neighborhoods, and the work usually consisted of cleaning up rubble for the reconstruction of neighborhood centers, YMCAs, etc.; and repairing school playgrounds, campgrounds, and the like. The voluntary service work camp experience was so positive that in the fall of 1948 MCC established a year-round work camp at Espelkamp, which anticipated some aspects of the Pax work.

This study/service work camp experience was not unique with the Mennonites. Other American colleges and relief organizations launched their own programs, especially in Germany, resulting in the formation of work camp associations.[12] But by 1950, the Mennonite study/service program had expanded into an international program, attracting increasing numbers of young people from many European countries such as Great Britain, France, Holland, Austria, and youth from as far away as Australia and Indonesia.[13]

European-Mennonite VS

The significance of the work camp program was not lost on European Mennonites who observed that this was an opportunity to relate to American Mennonite youth, a tangible and visible contribution to the rebuilding of Europe, an opening to reach out to many disillusioned European youth that were seeking answers, and even a stimulus toward recovering a witness to the peace position.[14]

With the help of MCC, a committee of representatives from the Dutch, German, French, and Swiss Mennonite churches with MCC as the fifth member, was formed in December 1950, at Frankfurt, Germany.[15] Consequently, *Mennonitsher Freiwilligendienst* (MFD), also known as Mennonite Voluntary Service (MVS), was born and became a semi-official cooperative organization of the four Mennonite churches in Holland, Germany, France, and Switzerland.[16]

After 1951, MVS sponsored an average of five to six camps per year in various countries, especially in Austria, Holland, and Germany, where the greatest war damage had been done.[17] The MFD-MVS program lasted into the late 1960s. To this day there are local residents who remember the community centers, student centers, small churches, and other institutions that received substantial assistance from an MFD international work camp. These projects can still be visited today if the traveler knows how to find them.[18]

Few if any American Mennonite youth who participated in the work camps had a good "pacifist" answer to the haunting question of how can a society solve the emergence of a dictator who had great vision and did many good things for the nation but who ostensibly became deranged and/or derailed. This dilemma often found German young people defending Hitler. Communism, which most North Americans agreed was diabolical but which helped defeat Hitler,[19] presented another ideological dilemma. Nevertheless the relationships that developed among the campers often matured into meaningful and life-long friendships; even some international marriages resulted.

The story of MFD/MVS, is a significant piece of history in its own right; many people in a variety of European communities recall the power and significance of the physical and psychological contribution made by the World War II work camp movement in general and MFD/MVS in particular. This Mennonite movement easily fit into the larger system of student and other youth exchanges from various religious denominations, national and international voluntary service organizations that formed a remarkably cosmopolitan little "League of Nations" movement in Europe.[20]

Indeed, beginning in 1950 the United Nations, under UNESCO, its educational and scientific wing, sponsored conferences to help the work of the camps. UNESCO also supported the formation of a European-wide "International Association of Work Camps" (*Arbeitsgemeinshaft Internationaler Arbeitslager*) which sponsored meetings and activities to encourage international work. MFD/MVS was an active member of this organization until MFD/MVS terminated.

As people worked in MVS projects, it became increasingly obvious that providing American college students with mind-expanding experiences and an opportunity to provide even small bits of material assistance only symbolized the vast almost unlimited opportunity for those young men in America who were about to be drafted. The MVS program expanded and continued to stimulate enthusiasm and vision among the European youth, as well as the Mennonite conferences in France, Holland, Germany, and Switzerland, especially as teams of MVS participants made visits to the churches and reported on what was happening.

Another strand in the development of the MVS program and Pax is the Espelkamp project referred to above. Espelkamp had been a poison gas munitions manufacturing plant during World War II. In June 1947, shortly after the war ended, "Birger Forell completed final arrangements for the release of the former munitions plant to the Evangelisches Hilsfwerk (EH) of the Protestant Churches in Germany."[21] This German relief agency was given the responsibility of converting the munitions bunkers into refugee housing. Each refugee was to provide his share of "self help" for a new home by preparing 2,000 cleaned and reusable bricks from the rubble of the destroyed barracks.

In December 1948, MCC established a voluntary service unit under the direction of Milton Harder to help the Evangelisches Hilfswerk by assisting refugees who were physically not able to do the work. Beyond this, the VS unit also was to engage in community development work. Emily Brunk observes that "Espelkamp has the distinction of being the only European M.C.C.-V.S. work camp which grew into a long term community program."[22] On occasion the camp had a number of European Mennonite volunteers. In addition to providing building assistance, the unit also conducted community service and development programs running the gamut from worship services and Sunday schools to boys/girls club activities and helping individual refugee families with specific building and renovation jobs.

After a number of years, MCC turned the project over to the Conservative Amish Mennonite Conference mission board, which then continued the social and religious emphases for a number of years.[23] In some significant aspects, the Espelkamp MCC VS unit was a precursor of the German Pax units and, as explained below, was the site for the first Mennonite refugee resettlement venture. The Pax program borrowed heavily from the VS structure. Similarities included a unit leader; a matron; a project foreman; volunteers from American and European countries serving for varied time periods; work on local projects involving contributions of labor in kind from the recipients; and unit activities in the community such as recreation, language classes, and youth work.

(above) The first group of Pax men, with " Pop" Swartzentruber, far right, minus Arnold Roth. Richard Rush photo.

(below) General Lewis Hershey (center) visiting the Espelkamp Pax unit. To the right of Hershey are Paul Peachey and H. A. Fast.
Photo courtesy Howard Landis

Chapter 3

Germination
of the Pax Idea

Modern mass media have jaded our sensitivities with incessant images of disasters, violence, genocide, revolutions, and wars that continue around the world. Nevertheless, all those who worked in Europe after World War II, regardless of affiliation, were overwhelmed by the massive destruction, the laceration of human families and communities, and the depressing pall of hopelessness that permeated the landscape. It is impossible for travelers in Europe today, if they did not see the destruction, to imagine what it looked like in the decade after 1944.

One of the most accessible descriptions, in text and pictures, of the tragedy and destruction of World War II is the October 1955 issue of *Mennonite Life*. The story line begins with "Europe on the Brink of Disaster," showing the horror of destroyed German cities, and ends with "Reconstruction in Germany." Appropriately, the latter shows pictures of the beginning of the Pax construction program. This, then, is the context of the beginnings of Pax.

The Idea of Foreign Service for Mennonite COs

In early August 1950, a group of Mennonite leaders from Europe met to discuss re-establishing a stable community life for the many refugees coming from the east temporarily housed in refugee camps in Germany. Returning to Frankfurt, Paul Peachey, then MCC director of special projects in Germany, and Calvin Redekop, director of MCC Voluntary Service, were discussing the importance and power of international exchange in giving Europe a new perspective. Peachey, reflecting on his reconstruction experience in Belgium from 1947 to 1948, and Redekop, full of enthusiasm derived from his work with the voluntary service camps, speculated how the hands-on aspect of the earlier builders units in France and Belgium, and the voluntary service work camps just completed in mid-summer, were a perfect way to combine the promotion of peace and practice of service.

In a moment of stimulating inspiration, they came to the simultaneous thought: "Why couldn't we get idealistic American young people to come to Europe to work at constructive projects such as refugee housing that would also broaden their horizons by meeting European young people and by confronting more directly the evils of war?" And with the looming threat of a larger war in Korea, and the potential of reinstatement of the draft in the United States, "might this not also fulfill the alternative to war service?"[1]

MCC soon brought Mennonite leaders to Frankfurt and they strongly supported the proposal. With these events in the background, Paul Peachey wrote O.O. Miller, executive secretary of MCC, on August 29, and stated that

> Yesterday we met with unofficial representatives of the Dutch, French, Swiss, and German Mennonites to counsel further about the possibility of a more concrete participation for European Mennonites in the program (VS). You will also note that we are thinking of an international Mennonite team of volunteers to help in the resettlement project of the West Prussian Mennonites in Germany. Brother Klassen and I have discussed this briefly a number of times and he has been eager for this kind of help once the resettlement projects reach that state. Our first attempt will be the small farm project at Uffweilerhof near Zweibruecken.

Peachey then wrote to relief director J. N. Byler on September 5, regarding the continuing and even expansion of the number of voluntary service workers for the reconstruction work at Espelkamp and elsewhere. He stated,

> With the world situation as it is we feel it would be highly desirable to keep a fairly well articulated V.S. program going as a possible alternative service. Certainly there

would be more chance of getting approval from the Governments on such a thing if we already had a good program in action. Right now because of initiative taken by the Bonn Government, the churches are negotiating with the Government regarding the position of conscientious objection. The Mennonites in Germany will need some encouragement to press for a satisfactory decision on this question and we feel that the program as we have now outlined it, will offer some possibilities.[2]

This letter implies two additional purposes for the proposed program. The first was to provide a model for the emerging pacifist sentiment in Europe and the second to encourage Mennonites to begin to think of nonresistance as a viable option since public opinion was beginning to turn toward denying war as the only way of solving world problems. After further discussions at Frankfurt, Calvin Redekop wrote a letter to O. O. Miller on November 24, 1950:

The big topic is the new international team which has been visualized and [now] activated as far as possible. I refer you to the copy of a memorandum which Paul Peachey sent to the Mennonite churches of the four European countries requesting the furnishing of representatives on a board that should activate voluntary service on an international Mennonite scale. In my report of the summer V.S. activities, I outlined the four reasons for their existence. This council has been set up and is now fairly active [the MVS/MFD program described above]. The main reason for the creation of this Council was to expeditiously and subtlety transfer part, and eventually all, of the responsibility of the Voluntary Service concept in Europe into their hands. We hope to have a continuous core of fellows from Holland, Switzerland, France, and Germany numbering from 15 to 20. This team or teams, if it becomes large enough to be divided, will be concerned directly with helping the refugee settlement program which Brothers Graber and Klassen are launching. The brethren, Graber and Klassen, see very clearly [agree with] the use of the camps in the refugee building program, not only to help the refugees build homes, but also to draw into the construction work many of the refugees who should be given responsibility in procuring their homes.[3]

The original idea was to establish an international voluntary service builders unit, which would be composed of European and American Mennonite young people, including American men who might get alternative service credit for it. Eventually it was hoped that alternative service might become a reality for European conscientious objectors as well. In his letter to Miller, Redekop continued,

> It goes without saying that the benefit to the American fellows in terms of a concept of service, plus the other benefits, would merit many a young fellow's service [of draft age] for several years. Two fellows from my home church [Bruderthaler Church in Mountain Lake, Minnesota] have been drafted into the army in the last two months. Barring the influence the church community should have given them I am sure if we could have offered them a year of service in Europe, helping in a critical cause, they would be here at the present time [rather than in the army].[4]

The Pax Idea Is Enacted

The idea had not gotten lost in the flurry of MCC's ongoing affairs, for on December 4, 1950, O. O. Miller replied to Redekop,

> Responding to your letter of the 24th, we note with much interest European VS development and planning and vision. We have noted too with particular interest the special VS European Danziger resettlement builder's unit, the outline of which has been suggested in a number of correspondence items crossing my desk within recent days.[5]

Miller continued,

> Our December 2 Executive Committee took note of this as per the following minute: Moved and passed to accept the following Executive Secretary's recommendation: that the Committee get ready and stand ready (1) to recruit up to 20 IV-E deferred single men into an European Danziger resettlement builder's unit; (2) the service to be for a year or more with qualification and allowance terms same as VS; (3) the unit to be supported from designated funds at $900 per year-worker; (4) the unit to be organized, assigned, and directed by the Assistant Executive Secretary.[6]

After having presented the plan to, and gaining approval from, the executive committee on December 2, 1950, the plan was presented to the MCC annual meeting and was approved on March 15, 1951. This was an amazing feat.[7]

In the meantime, before MCC's full board had even given its final approval, publicity for the program was released and young men responded. They were processed, the financial and logistical arrangements were made, travel was arranged, and they arrived in Europe within four months. A peace "army" had been mobilized on foreign soil with a gestation period of less than five months—a rather presumptuous and preposterous idea, and an even more unlikely realization in such a short time! But the European MCC workers had challenged headquarters that if MCC would send the "boys," MCC personnel in Europe would arrange for the projects and manage them.[8] This amazing development probably provides the best insight into the entire Pax saga, a remarkably idealistic, naive, flexible, experimental, and ingenious jerry-built dream. And it was brought to life with an equally vast amount of vigor, vitality, and energy resulting from the synergism of a number of idealistic sources converging at a single point in time.

Groundwork for the Pax Program

But how was it possible that a request for some American men to help in refugee reconstruction and the formation of a builders unit actually involved in home construction could have taken place almost instantaneously? To understand this, we need to remember that three major social and political actions were taking place on the world scene: the World War II refugee problem, Germany's desperate economic conditions, and the draft in the United States. Fortuitously, or some would say providentially, these issues contributed to the quick birth of Pax.[9]

The economic crises had been intensely discussed among the world community of nations on political, social, and even military levels. The tragic refugee situation in Germany and neighboring nations was demanding international attention. On August 2, 1950, William Snyder wrote O. O. Miller stating that

ECA (the Economic Cooperation Administration) is moving vigorously toward the resettlement of German refugees in western Germany. The reason for this seems obvious as the recent elections in Germany have pointed out the tremendous power, politically, of the refugees and the need for finding homes in which they can be content. Our Danzig Mennonites problem must be coordinated with this ECA help and I am afraid we will not get the most effective assistance if we depend on Bonn officials [alone].[10]

There was at the same time considerable international concern to settle refugees in other countries. In an MCC executive committee meeting in September 1950, O. O. Miller said that

Brother C. L. Graber, brother C.F. Klassen and I met in Washington with the State Department and Economic Cooperation Administration. The subject was the Danzig Mennonite question. We learned that the E.C.A. is taking more seriously its social responsibility in meeting the problems of Western Germany. There were two principal parts to our discussion. A. A possible movement of 750 persons to Uruguay with E.C.A. financial assistance. B. Resettlement of Danzig Mennonites in Western Germany.[11]

On October 6, 1950, the Executive Committee "moved and passed [the motion] that C. L. Graber, churchman and businessman from Goshen, Indiana, be appointed to service of six months or more in Europe as special assistant to C. F. Klassen to help Danzig resettlement in Germany."[12] William Snyder believed that

the C. L. Graber appointment by the Executive Committee will move us much farther along in our western Europe resettlement work. I believe our stakes must be wider than the two projects, which the Executive Committee has already approved even though these two may require much of his attention during his six month term. It would seem equally important that Brother Graber's ability in carrying negotiations with government, particularly American Government officials [presumably meaning here American officials in Germany] be used to utmost advantage.[13]

The story of C. L. Graber's arrival in Europe in October 1950, and the work he did to arrange for the financial and governmental agencies continues below. At the time the first Pax men were solicited and processed, no one knew whether the United States government would give alternative service credit for the service, how the organization would be structured and financed, or what the builders would do once they got to Europe, if in fact the myriad agreements and permissions could be arranged for the ambitious and utopian goals. But they were, surprising both MCC workers in Europe and the MCC executive committee who were well aware of the bureaucratic and traditional norms that applied to European institutions.

Simultaneously, with the rebuilding of Germany and the resettlement of refugees, there had been ongoing discussions with Selective Service, via the National Service Board for Religious Objectors (NSBRO), regarding alternative service recognition for the draftees in the face of the Korean War. This accelerated the origins and birth of Pax.[14]

The various parts of the vague and amorphous but grand vision began to fall in place. MCC had dispatched Chris Graber to Europe to work with the German government and the Allied High Commission and secure the release of "blocked funds" held in Zurich[15] paid for by the Mennonite Central Committee. These monies became a revolving loan fund for the construction of refugee housing in a number of locations where refugees from Danzig were being temporarily housed in refugee camps or in scattered farmsteads. The refugees would then repay the loans over thirty-four years.

As if divinely foreordained, the role the Pax men were supposed to play became a critical reality. During the negotiations, the German banks maintained that the refugees would need to provide a ten percent downpayment toward the cost of the houses before the project could be approved. C. L. Graber asked whether work-in-kind on the construction of the houses would be counted as contribution toward the downpayment. The answer was positive, and Graber confidently said this would be no problem.

Where would he get this help? Graber, in the typically American "can do" style, which had characterized him all his life, said young men from America would provide the work.

He did not tell the negotiators that nary a one would have any building experience but assumed that American boys were made of the "right stuff."

Graber happily agreed when the authorities insisted that a professional German building contractor serve as overseer for each project. The arrangement would preclude complications with the bureaucratic German building system including codes and standards as well as protection against possible complications later regarding procedures or inadequacy of construction.[16] It is difficult to imagine the complexities and complications of setting up construction projects and the manpower to run them in a foreign country, which was literally unable to function because its infra-structure was in shambles.

Yet while the infrastructure was inoperable, the traditional cultural norms and institutions were still in force. The first reconstruction project at Espelkamp is a perfect case study, but no record of the negotiations is easily available, if extant.

Only one aspect of the negotiations, taken from the author's personal experience, can be recounted here. After arrangements with the German government and ECA had been made for the Espelkamp project, an MVS team was assigned to convert poison gas bunkers to dormitories for the Pax team. In the meantime, however, the county's permission and arrangements to fell the trees to make way for the project had not been processed at the local office (Lübbecke).[17]

The Paxers Arrive

The first Pax team arrived on April 6, at Espelkamp, and settled in a newly renovated gas munitions bunker. The team was waiting on the site for a number of days but, without permission to cut trees, there was nothing for them to do. Morale was hanging precariously on a slender thread when Redekop, the inexperienced but assertive Pax director, called C. F. Klassen and told him what he was going to do. Klassen concurred. So the men took the Dodge Power Wagon and proceeded to pull down some of the stately pines with the wagon's powerful winch.[18] In the meantime, Redekop had dispatched one of the Pax men to Lübbecke to tell forestry officials that the Paxers were beginning to remove the trees. Peter

Neufeld noted in his diary that

> MCC provided a Dodge Power Wagon with a winch in
> front. We used it to pull out the stumps. We chained the
> back end to a stump and hooked the front cable to another
> tree stump and then tromped on the gas. I was surprised
> that the Power Wagon was not pulled into pieces.[19]

Within several hours after a number of trees had been up-
rooted, a group of German officials were on the scene. A tense
discussion took place, but after the authorities were convinced
that Pax men had come to stay and help build refugee homes,
they relented. Later the local government officials and the Pax
unit became good friends, and today's Espelkamp residents
proudly retell the story of the "Pax boys."

Almost every early Pax project, not only in Germany, but
elsewhere has its own unique story to tell of how each project
began and how local practices and traditions had to be taken
into consideration in order to incarnate the new vision.[20] For
example, Harry Harder, the MCC director of the Trans-Chaco
road project, and his team of seven Pax men, stopped at the
Caterpillar plant at Peoria, Illinois, on their way to Asuncion,
Paraguay, for a crash course in maintenance and operation of
these huge machines. After they landed in Asuncion, they
faced a local version of the red tape which took weeks running
into months, to unravel.[21]

The Algerian project faced complicated jurisdictional issues. As Gary Mullet, another Pax man explained, "Algeria is
divided into departments. The administrative center of each
department is called a prefecture, divided into arrondisse-
ments each with its own center—a subprefecture."[22] Unexpected program shifts also complicated matters. After the project, opened in 1962, the program soon changed its direction
from focusing on local illiterate farmers to more broad community development. Gary found himself leading a vaccina-
tion course against African horse disease. He stated, "I enjoy
working around horses. But I wasn't trained for this. It's hard
when you have just bits and pieces of knowledge."[23]

The completed Backnang project, taken by US Army Signal Corps.
Courtesy *Mennonite Weekly Review*

(above) The Karlsschule, Vienna, Austria, joint Brethren-Mennonite work project.
Courtesy Brethren Encyclopedia Collection at the Brethren Historical Library
and Archives, Elgin, Illinois

(below) Pax Chorus, Germany, 1955
Courtesy Mennonite Central Committee photo collection,
Archives of the Mennonite Church (hereafter MCC-AMC)

Chapter 4

Launching
the Pax Program

The optimistic spirit of recovery energizing North American society and economics after the devastation of World War II seemed to rub off on Mennonites as well. Reflecting on the state of American Mennonites at the close of World War II, Paul Toews opined that

> More and more ideology, servant activism and volunteerism were replacing cultural markers as the central carriers of Mennonite peoplehood. That generation was moving the church toward a more clearly defined theology of service and a more globally engaged missional activity.[1]

An aspect of this new Mennonite ethos of international service was beginning to take shape and its name was *Pax*.

Recruiting the Volunteers

The general administrative responsibility for the new international Pax effort was lodged in the MCC relief section, which was directly responsible to the executive secretary, O. O. Miller by way of Assistant Executive Secretary William T. Snyder. From the European perspective, however, there were additional lines of responsibility, as shown below. The call for volunteers went out to the churches, as did requests for $900 support per year for housing and board, transportation to and from Europe, and incidental costs. The full contingent of twenty young men between ages nineteen and twenty-one did materialize, along with later commitments of $1,080 per year from sending families or congregations.

The events that led to the announcements regarding the program and the way in which the men responded to the call are relatively obscure and buried in archives or in the memories of the Pax men. The church papers carried announcements of the proposed program, and MCC personnel visited a variety of meetings and conferences to introduce the program. The motivations of the men volunteering for the first group and the subsequent projects obviously varied as the times changed. Howard Landis, a member of the first Pax unit reports that

> My teens had been a time of turmoil. So I became another young person searching for meaning. I did a lot of reading, including the Bible. Some months after I made a religious commitment, life took on meaning and I began to see some direction and purpose. Shortly after I saw a note about the Builders Unit program planned to help refugees in Germany. The idea struck a responsive chord, so I applied. I suspect the men in the first Builders Unit were indulging in an urge for adventure and change, they were frontier personalities. These first men were true pioneers.[2]

Pondering why he had responded to the appeal for Pax recruits, Earl Martin says,

> Perhaps it was the missionaries in our home telling exciting stories about their work. Or maybe it was the current events classes at Maple Grove when we talked about Australia and the Suez. Maybe it was the letters from my brother Luke in Germany [in Pax]. It could have been the foreign exchange students in high school or college. Whatever it was, I had known for a long time that someday I would go.[3]

Pax took Earl to Vietnam, and it changed his life.

In retrospect, the Pax men's arrival in Antwerp on April 6, 1951 seems to have been the culmination of a preposterous dream. Scarcely six months earlier the idea of sending young men to war-ravaged Germany to rebuild homes for refugees had been submitted to the executive secretary of the Mennonite Central Committee in Akron, Pennsylvania. Now Redekop and Paul Ruth of Menno Travel Service in Amsterdam were at the dockside to meet the young men. Mostly farm boys, they were ready and waiting, having volunteered to help build refugee homes, not knowing whether their service would be recognized by the Selective Service System as alternative service to military duty.

The Selective Service and Pax Men

But developing events would ultimately serve the purposes of the Pax men. On June 19, 1951, some two months after the Paxers arrived in Europe, the US Congress passed the "Universal Military Training and Service Act." The Act made the Selective Service agency a permanent one, ended the deferment of conscientious objectors and required that "the CO shall be ordered by his local board, subject to such regulations as the President may prescribe to perform such civilian work contributing to the maintenance of the national health, safety, or interest as the local board may deem appropriate."[4]

The Selective Service program had learned a lot from the experience of World War II. The CPS organization and program had not been totally successful. The new program, called the "Conscientious Objector Work Program" had its

> beginning shortly after the outbreak of the Korean conflict when strong public sentiments developed that some form of service be required of those registrants who were opposed to both combatant and noncombatant service and who, at the time, were given statuary deferments.[5]

Congress approved the alternative service, but Victor Olson states,

> Having legislated the bare outlines of a plan for using this manpower, the Congress promptly withdrew from the scene leaving to the Executive Branch the matter of carrying out this rather nebulous mandate. When it became evident that all of the federal agencies were not interested, it was decreed by the President that the Selective Service System add this sensitive assignment to its other responsibilities.

According to Olson the major difference between the CPS program and the I-W program was that "The program today operates on a decentralized basis and deals almost exclusively with the conservation of human resources as opposed to the program of World War II which typified central control and a concern with the conservation of natural resources."[6]

Whether the I-W program was proving any more successful and meaningful was widely debated. The entire July 1958 issue of *Mennonite Life* is devoted to the history and development nature of the draft regulations and the implications for Mennonites and other peace groups. But Olson's phrase, "the conservation of human resources," is central to the Pax vision and clearly allowed the Pax idea more latitude.

Foreign Service Approval

However, the phrase "contribute to the national health, safety or interest" certainly seemed to preclude foreign service. Further, giving local draft boards the power to decide where COs could serve could help make the Act an impossible bureaucratic nightmare. But the phrase "harmless as doves, but wise as serpents" was not unknown among Mennonites. Prior to World War II, Mennonites had aggressively participated in gaining legal recognition for pacifists and Mennonite representatives became well known to Congress. Through the MCC, Mennonites had strongly supported establishing a "lobbying office" for the National Service Board for Religious Objectors.[7] So an appeal was made via the NSBRO for an exception clause to allow COs to serve abroad. (See Appendix B for details.)

The appeal was noted, and General Lewis B. Hershey, who had been in charge of the CO program during World War II was dispatched to Europe in August 1951, to investigate the program. In a letter to Pax pastor A. Lloyd Swartzentruber, European director H. A. Fast informed him of the impending visit, noting that

> One of the primary purposes of General Hershey's visit is to explore the possibility of permitting men classified as IV-E to serve in foreign areas under the draft act. He has now written that he will land at Bremerhaven August 5 and will soon after that be available to visit with us our Pax Service Units.[8]

Hershey subsequently visited the builders units at Espelkamp, saw the refugee houses going up (only the foundations), traveled Neuwied, and visited MCC headquarters in Basel, Switzerland, as well as several other church relief agencies. He returned to the United States to give unqualified approval to the program as eligible for alternate service to military duty on foreign soil. Hershey's positive stance could be attributed at least in part to the fact that he was a third-generation descendant of the peaceful Mennonites.[9]

The process of accreditation for alternative service, however, was agonizingly slow. On July 21, 1952, Pax director Redekop finally could write,

Dear Pax Fellows:

By now most of you should have received a sheaf of letters from Dave Karber giving you latest information about Selective Service developments and requesting signature and return of two letters to your draft boards. You should be aware that as developments now stand you will not receive alternative service credit until your draft board receives the letters Dave requested you to sign. Upon this the draft board will complete forms 151-2-3, and there upon present you with a I-W classification.

It is possible that a draft board may not even grant I-W upon receipt of a request for classification because they may not as yet have received the official blanks for 1-0 from Selective Service headquarters, and before they get these they will not award I-Ws. There is not much we can do about speeding up Selective Service but we should not be guilty of letting things drag that are within our power.[10]

In the first group of Pax men, most of whom stayed one year, some received credit upon returning home while others were given no alternative credit. Some of the fellows who stayed on in Europe beyond their first year (April 1951-April 1952) received credit from the time the act was passed, others were given credit retroactively from April 1, while still a few others had to begin anew and work in alternative service assignments when they returned to the United States.

The differences stemmed from the attitudes of local Selective Service boards who had the power to grant or deny conscientious objector status. Each board reacted on the basis of the local conditions, which naturally reflected the community attitudes toward the so called "unpatriotic" groups known as the "peace churches." However, there was generally high esteem for groups such as the Church of the Brethren, the Quakers, the Mennonites, and the Jehovah's Witnesses, the groups with the largest proportion choosing the pacifist position. This also helped determine the chances of being given CO status.

Seven years later, Hershey returned to Europe to evaluate the effectiveness of the Pax program. He traveled to the Karlsschule Unit in Vienna on September 9-10. He then visited the Enkenbach Pax project, Bad Duerkheim, and Kaiserslautern on November 3, 1959.[11] According to Peter Dyck, Hershey had no reservations. Speaking in parables of sharing bread with the poor, Hershey said that

> There is no need to talk and to explain. This is obvious. It's like that here with Enkenbach. I can understand this kind of language. There are some programs with a lot of talk and a great deal of explanation. Maybe that is why I appreciate what the Mennonites are doing, because even I can understand without any explanation what the giving of bread and the building of houses means.[12]

Several years later, while at the twentieth anniversary meeting of the National Service Board for Religious Objectors (NSBRO), Hershey is said to have stated, "These men of Karlsschule and elsewhere are examples of what one should be to represent the United States abroad. The standards set by these men will be hard to meet by the Peace Corps being advocated by President John F. Kennedy."[13]

According to the records, there was no further evaluation of Pax by the Selective Service System. The entire operation was apparently satisfactory and, as indicated by Hershey, so concretely meeting human needs that it could not be misinterpreted or misunderstood.

Preparing for the Long Haul

This multi-faceted and organic series of events marked the beginning of what became known as Pax Services. Church papers recruited young conscientious objectors from among all the groups across the spectrum of Mennonite communities and conferences. In one such appeal, a church leader said,

> There is a need for a clear witness to the power of Christ in the world and in every area of life because of the sin, ignorance, poverty and disillusionment in which people are living. . . . Communism offers its solution to the people of the world, but what does the Christian have to offer?[14]

Congregations supported the young men they sent with a monthly fee of $75. By 1963 this was raised to $90 per month, with the two-year assignment costing a total of $2,160. Each Pax man received a personal spending allowance of $15 per month.

The young volunteers, mostly with high school educations, were brought to Akron, Pennsylvania, for fifteen days of "service orientation and instructions."[15] This curriculum included Mennonite church history, MCC history, Christian nonresistance, peace witness, the meaning of sacrificial services, and cultural adjustments.

With this sincere yet obviously hasty preparation the men were destined to be flexible and resourceful. By default they were prepared to expect an unlimited variety of unstructured conditions about which they had no or little advance information. Paradoxically, however, the men were extremely unprepared to respond to the variety of needs the Pax program addressed as it emerged from its beginnings in 1951.

Yet in another sense, the Paxers were superbly prepared, because they were told to see their service as "a means of self-development, [since] working in intimate contact with people of other backgrounds, the dedicated worker will broaden his own personality and understanding." The *Pax Handbook* further indicated that the Pax volunteer's purpose was "to promote international goodwill and understanding through the total impact of the program by working with citizens of other countries in a spirit of sharing and brotherly love."[16]

The Ambiguous Status of Pax

The wholistic, diffused, and even "charismatic" nature of the Pax program is reflected in the fact that it never had a clear structural niche in the MCC organizational structure. Indeed, within MCC, the philosophy regarding Pax was a marvel of crossing lines of authority and its operation was very convoluted.[17] Pax was "never intended as a separate section or department of overseas service. It has been seen as a unique way to use capable, available persons within a total program of MCC relief and rehabilitation work."[18] Furthermore, there was no clear vision as to the status of Pax and the European MVS program (see Appendix D).

So just before the first Pax group arrived, a meeting of European MCC administrators called a meeting in Frankfurt in March 29, 1951, to "plan together for carrying forward the resettlement and the Builders' Unit programs." It was agreed that the

> Builders Unit (Pax Services) is set up directly under the Executive Secretary of MCC at Akron. . . . Since Pax Services One will need to cooperate with MCC Relief Section for food, vehicles, etc. and with International Voluntary Service Program for leadership in organization and administration, Cal Redekop will cooperate with C. F. Klassen in planning and administering Pax Services One program and shall be the person through whom coordination between these programs is worked out.
>
> It is understood that while Akron thinks of Pax Services One as a separate and distinct program and some will be administered that way, yet International Voluntary Service can consider Pax Services as one phase of the IVS program and furnish personnel to work with Pax Services One provided that if they live with Pax Services One, they be subject to same discipline and that proper accounting be set up to keep clear and separate the support and maintenance costs.[19]

But the original proposal from Europe did not coincide with the view from headquarters at Akron and for a time an uneasy relationship prevailed. Finally on April 9, 1952, O. O. Miller wrote Redekop,

> We here at Akron do consider MCC Pax Services and the European VS distinctly different in concept, purpose, goals, and in administrative implementation. We hope that European VS could be guided by the same concepts, goals and purposes that guide North American MCC VS but this in the fine points is not essential from the fact that European VS and North American MCC VS have no organic relation-

ship to each other whatever. Pax services was conceived originally by MCC Executive Committee as an experiment for using abroad deferred 4-E classified single men only. The only change in concept to this point is that under the new law we will think of it as services abroad for I-W single men. I hope I have answered clearly enough so that you can accept it as a satisfactory answer to your letter of March 31.[20]

The letter from Miller concluded, "It will be helpful to you in your assignment and responsibilities if you think and work closely with us in these several endeavors and experiments."[21] Research has revealed no information on why the Akron officials were so hesitant about allowing Pax men and MVS persons to work together. But Pax consisted of young men, barely over eighteen years of age, so the idea of mixing with European young people, especially co-ed in some cases, could easily have raised serious concerns about constituency support as well as Selective Service System approval.

Whatever the reasons, the envisioned structural cooperative relationship with European Mennonites via the robust Mennonite Voluntary Service program was attenuated if not ultimately stifled. Consequently the possibility of a future international voluntary service organization, which would serve conscientious objectors from various countries, was truncated.

It is impossible to know if such a model would have evolved, but given contemporary realities in Europe in which Mennonites now can claim military service exemption in several countries, it might have been realized.[22] In any case, the Pax Services program and the European MVS program continued to work hand in glove in an interdependent relationship for a number of years.

The decisions regarding the relationships between MVS and Pax, as well as decisions regarding projects which moved beyond the refugee settlement activities, continued to be a point of contention between the Akron office and the European Pax office. On March 19, 1952, William T. Snyder wrote a letter suggesting "a departure of Pax into fields other than organized builders units." Redekop replied on March 31, 1952 that

There is no question that the project Grace Rhodes recommends which was inspired by Pastor Mensching is a good one. We are acquainted with this [project]. There are however many other projects which we know about here on the field which, judged by many different premises, may be just as important. There remains a question whether the decision on where Pax could best serve should not emanate form the field since we have opportunity to discriminate between various possibilities.[23]

There is, however, a certain intrigue in the way the International Mennonite Voluntary Service vision persisted despite official MCC headquarters' efforts to control the Pax program. Many of the Pax projects had participants from the local recipient communities. For example, the Paraguayan Trans-Chaco road building unit included volunteers from the Chaco, Friesland, and Volendam colonies, as did the Bechterdiessen, Vienna, Salzburg, and other units. Of course these volunteers were not processed through Akron, and had to obtain their own support from local sponsoring persons or agencies. But the practical effects were much the same: an international Mennonite voluntary service movement.

The Pax program in Europe, was administered from its office in Frankfurt Germany until the major building programs were completed. But beginning in 1953, as is obvious or implicit in the descriptions of the various programs in other parts of the world, the Akron office assigned all the other Pax men. Therefore the self-conscious *esprit de corps* that evolved in the European projects did not extend to the other units. To this day, many Pax European men are hardly aware that Pax also existed in other countries.[24]

(above) Randy Schertz discussing plants with club member in Brasil, 1970. MCC-AMC

(below) Paul Delegrange with Liberian men demonstrating chicken program, 1960. MCC-AMC

Chapter 5

The Major Pax Projects

The first Pax unit arrived in Espelkamp in the state of Nord Rhein-Westfalen in early April to serve "in the name of Christ." It is hard to imagine a more powerful symbolic response to the call of Micah to God's people to "turn swords into plowshares and spears into pruning hooks" for Espelkamp had been the site for the production and storage of bombs and poison gas.

> From 800 to 1,000 people worked here constructing and assembling grenades, rocket bombs, and gas bombs; girls worked in three, eight-hour shifts sewing the fuses and filling shells with powder, their skins turning yellow from the powerful chemicals. Throughout the woods there were smaller camouflaged halls and 22 bunkers in which raw products and the finished armaments were stored. To the far west, barracks were erected as living quarters for Russian prisoners of war. S.S. troops, and the Deutsche Jugend.[1]

Espelkamp had been designed and built to kill.

Upon arrival, Howard Landis, a member of the first group wrote his parents,

> We made a tour through Espelkamp and it was extremely interesting. It was so camouflaged that not a bomb was dropped on it [during the war]. There were many little masonry bunkers that had been built to store poison gas. When the Germans build something, they build it good. They are now using these buildings for homes.[2]

When Allies discovered Espelkamp at the end of the war the production facilities were quickly destroyed. But now it was to become the site for building houses for the homeless.

Strangely, one prisoner of war had heard of Espelkamp, and suggested,

> that [rather than being destroyed] such a place [that is the barracks] could be used more profitably to house some of the 12,000,000 refugees uprooted through the terrible years just passed. [With the permission of the Allies], and [with] the cooperation of the Hilsfwerk of the Protestant Churches in Germany, the machinery was set in motion that eventually rescued Espelkamp from the Allied destruction program.[3]

On this basis, cooperative planning between the German officials and MCC had determined that the complex could be transformed into a major refugee settlement community. A part of the first Pax unit was soon dispatched to Neuwied to produce cinder blocks for housing construction at Espelkamp and later for Neuwied itself.[4]

The Character and Variety of the Projects

In a very short time, the German building inspector arrived at the Espelkamp site in north Germany. His reactions, when he put the "boys" to work and discovered most had no "specialized" building experience according to traditional German expectations, can be imagined. But the Pax director's passionate appeal to "give the boys a chance" avoided a potential crisis, and the "boys" soon demonstrated that they could learn fast.

The original mandate to build refugee houses in Germany expanded from the original projects at Espelkamp and Neuwied to six locations, including Backnang, Wedel, Enkenbach, and Bechterdiessen, respectively.[5] Backnang, the third major project, was conducted in two phases, the first comprised of sixty-six family units, completed in 1954, and the second made up of forty family units completed several years later.[6]

By 1958, Pax men had built more than 400 houses for refugees. An exact count of the number of homes built and families settled is not available and may never have been tallied. The families who were to receive the homes were expected to provide 2,000 hours of labor. This was basically supplied by the Pax men, but all the families felt a moral obligation to provide labor. When physically possible, most of them gave as much time as they could and a sense of affinity and comradeship often developed on the work project as well as in informal social events. Lasting relationships were formed and then sustained with continuing visits between the refugee families and the American Pax men who later had families of their own.

The Pax experiment became a physical reality, which resulted in broad social and spiritual consequences. At one dedication ceremony, the leader of a German refugee relief organization said,

> The real and indispensable help of the Paxmen cannot be minimized. As we know and repeat today as we have before, none of the settlements could have been established if the Pax boys had not contributed the last notch in the financing, that is the "Eigenhilfe"(the self-help ten percent downpayment) which none of the refugees could have supplied.[7]

But almost immediately, other "emergencies" or needy projects were calling for Pax help. It did not take long for the Frankfurt office to assign Pax men to a variety of other projects. A major flood took place in Holland in 1953, so eleven Pax men were sent to join the MVS group who

> helped the stricken by traveling from village to village cleaning up debris, cleaning streets, tearing down damaged houses and cleaning up some of the destroyed ones. [For example] In Niewe Tonge, a village of 3,000, floods destroyed one-sixth of the houses and 85 people lost their lives. Pax helped in the construction of 12 pre-fabricated houses which were a gift to Holland from the Finnish Red Cross.[8]

By September 1954, eighty-eight Pax men were serving in seven European countries—sixty-seven in Germany, twelve in Greece, three in Holland, one each in Paris, Baghdad, Egypt, and Jericho.[9]

In 1955, a Pax group was sent to Kaiserslautern to build a community center. Also in 1955, a group of Pax men went to repair the bombed out Karlsschule in Vienna. The former

Protestant school was serving as a depot for distribution of food and supplies for refugees coming from the east after the war. This interesting project was originally begun by the Brethren Service Commission and Pax men worked together with the Brethren I-W men until the project was completed in April 1, 1961. According to Garber, a total of 127 men served there.[10] In 1957, a Pax group also helped build a church center in Krefeld.

By 1958, Pax men were sent to Berlin to help the Red Cross in a variety of ways from supervising recreation and libraries to construction and renovation of camp buildings for the burgeoning refugee population coming from the east. These spin-offs from the builders units were easily administered from Pax's Frankfurt headquarters, since most of them were projects initiated by MVS and subsequently jointly conducted.

Pax men were also assigned to Mennonite Voluntary Service to assist with a variety of other projects, such as helping arrange for work camp sites and to work in Jordan under the MCC and United Nations Relief and Rehabilitation Administration (UNRRA) refugee programs. In addition, several Pax men were assigned to the United Nations Educational and Scientific and Cultural Organization (UNESCO) international work camp headquarters in Paris, France, for a number of years.

In 1956 and 1957, more than fifteen Pax men were assigned to work with refugees in refugee camps after the 1956 Hungarian uprising. MCC opened three refugee camps, two in December 1956, and one in January 1957, all in the vicinity of Vienna. These were manned by Pax men from German units, under their own leadership. One camp operated for 178 days, the second for 130 days, and the third to be opened lasted for 166 days, until the refugees were all settled in other countries.[11]

Pax Expands Beyond Builders Units

But the Pax program was soon called to move beyond the German refugee theater and serve other communities in a serious way. The versatility of the Pax concept, the organization, and the men themselves continued to catch the imagination. Requests for their service were soon coming from all directions. Through MCC's global network, news of Pax reached Greece. In response, the Greek Orthodox Church asked Pax to help in agricultural rehabilitation in the Macedonia community of Panayitsa, which had been destroyed by the civil war between the communists and the Greek government.

So in April 1952, a unit of five men in a Chevrolet Suburban pulling a trailer loaded with supplies left the Pax headquarters in Frankfurt, Germany, and traveled through Austria and Yugoslavia to Greece. This Pax group was commissioned to help rebuild a rural agricultural community and help the farmers to reestablish farm production after the war had destroyed the animals and the land. The Pax men also ended up helping to re-establish the local school and the local government. In this project, what the men lacked in technical training and expertise they made up for in practical know-how, common sense, and meaningful and genuine interpersonal relationship. Again, many life-long friendships were formed.

As the idea of Pax grew, however, the office in Frankfurt was no longer able to serve the worldwide Pax efforts. The Pax program's expansion into other parts of the globe also changed the nature of Pax. As the Pax service idea expanded to encircle the world, the non-European projects were administered from the Akron office.

The global mission of Pax was launched in September 1951, when three men under the direct supervision of the MCC office[12] in Akron, Pennsylvania, left for eastern Paraguay to help with the wheat growing experiments directed by Servico Tecnico Inter-Americana Cooperacion Agricola (STICA). Later the Pax men were transferred to west Paraguay to participate in building the trans-Chaco highway. According to Gerhard Ratzlaff's account, twenty-nine men served in Paraguay from 1952 to 1968.[13]

In the fall of 1952, several Paxers went to Jordan to help MCC in its relief work, an effort that continued through 1969. In the first years, these men were supervised from Frankfurt. In 1953, two men left for Korea, which had just entered a debilitating struggle with North Korea. Pax men were stationed there until 1969, assisting in relief work directed by MCC. In all, at least forty men served there, usually for three years. Also in 1953, a group of Pax men went to Cairo, Egypt, to help with rural development projects there. Two years later Pax men began going to the Congo, encountering troubled times, as will be indicated below.[14]

Ten Pax men were sent to Peru in 1954 to serve at Tournavista, the project conducted by earth mover R.G. LeTourneau, who had a contract with the Peruvian government to build several roads. Around thirty-five young men served there for two- or three-year terms. Pax men went to Algeria in 1954 to help MCC in the relief and rehabilitation work after the earthquake of August 1954.

Nepal became the beneficiary of Pax men in 1956. The men helped in construction work, served in various positions in a local hospital, and were seconded to United Mission to Nepal, an interdenominational Christian organization. Pax men went to Vietnam in 1957; Morocco beginning in 1958; and faraway Asia, including Afghanistan, Pakistan, India, and Indonesia. By 1969, Pax men were serving in thirty-nine countries and several other countries were added after 1969.[15]

The variety and breadth of the Pax program has not even been fully grasped by Pax men themselves, much less rank and file Mennonites. The Bolivian program illustrates Pax's variety and exotic nature. The program began in 1961 and placed Pax men in a wide range of projects. These included helping MCC serve the social and community needs of the Old Colony Mennonites south of Santa Cruz, helping the Quechua Indians move from the Alto Plano to be resettled in the jungles of central Bolivia, working with Church of the Brethren Heifer projects, and serving as veterinarians.

At least seventy-five Pax men served in the Bolivia program. The unit was formally based in the Santa Cruz MCC center, and after the first Pax director, Art Driedger, returned to North America, the program was directed by MCCers Mary Willms and Mary Ann Epp respectively, nurses stationed in Santa Cruz. There was little unit life; instead most of the Pax fellows, stationed in the areas where they were assigned related to the several other persons involved in the same activities. On occasion, however, the Pax men met at the MCC center for special activities.[16]

Tabulations of Pax Projects

Is there any way of knowing what has been the exact amount and variety of work that the Pax men contributed through the years? Probably not, but some statistical information is available and summarized below. Table 1 presents the broad overview of the years and the number of men that served in Pax each year, followed by the number and names of countries in which projects were operative, and finally the countries in which programs were ended (completed). But these figures refer only to the larger projects where some type of unit life could be maintained. An exact tabulation of all the projects in which Pax men served is difficult to obtain since many Pax men, such as Carl Jantzen who went to Iraq, were assigned on an individual basis directly from Akron.

Table 1. Worldwide Service of Pax[17]

Year	Number Serving	Number/countries/project ended[18]
1951	31	1—Germany, Paraguay
1952	50	4—Greece, Jordan
1953	94	8—France, Holland, Korea, Egypt
1954	107	9—Peru
1955	106	11—Austria, Congo,
1956	109	15—Nepal, Algeria, Belgium, Indonesia
1957	104	16—Vietnam
1958	100	17—Morocco/Holland completed
1959	85	18—Liberia[19]
1960	87	22—Chile, Hong Kong, Pakistan, Thailand,
1961	102	27—Crete, Bolivia, British Honduras, India, Austria
1962	98	27— Burundi/ Thailand completed
1963	78	28— Israel
1964	89	30— West Pakistan, East Pakistan
1965	88	30—
1966	122	30—Nigeria/ Greece completed
1967	138	35—Mexico, Madagascar, Zambia, Yugoslavia, Dominican Republic/Hong Kong completed
1968	123	36—Haiti
1969	96	39—Brazil, Vietnam, Nepal
1970	124	40—Botswana
1971	87	42—Poland
1972	40	NA[20]
1973	46	

1974   24
1975   25

Sources: Urie Bender, *Soldiers of Compassion; Euro-Pax News*, MCC Annual Reports; MCC Files; miscellaneous documents and correspondence.

It is interesting to note that after 1954, the number of Pax men was relatively stable, until 1966, when it suddenly increased. This is undoubtedly related to the fact that the United States sent 184,000 combat soldiers into Vietnam in 1965.[21] The final number of men who served in Pax has not been finally established, but the names of about 1,180 men have been documented. If we assume these men served for two years, we come up with a figure of 2,360 "man years" of service.[22]

The Pax program, organization, and operations closed rather quietly in 1975. At the MCC executive board meetings of December 10-11, the action under personnel services states, "It was decided to discontinue the 'Pax' designation in subsequent appointments [subsequent presumably meaning projects where Pax fellows had been assigned earlier]."[23] The last Pax fellow to have been listed under the "Pax Service" rubric in the Executive Committee minutes as having gone into service was Russell Toews, of Whitewater, Kansas, who went to Bangladesh beginning November 6, 1975.[24]

A perspective on the variety and amount of the work the men did is best achieved by looking at the type of projects, where they were located, and when the projects were established.[25] Only the major projects involving a contingent of more than about four Pax workers have been tabulated. This table describes Pax endeavors, which addressed a large project demanding considerable manpower. These projects resulted in the formation of Pax residential units with all the attendant organizational aspects described later. The many special assignments involving one to three Pax men or more for a shorter period, can not be listed here but some are alluded to below.

Joint MVS/Pax projects, such as the Netherlands flood cleanup of June 1953, the Krefeld, Germany church center project, or the construction of the Mennonite church at Witmarsum, Netherlands, have not been included. It is doubtful that a total account of all of the various special projects is available.

Table 2. The Major Pax Undertakings[26]

Name/Location	Date	Type of Project Begun
Espelkamp, Germany	1951	Construction of refugee housing approximately 50 family units constructed
Neuwied, Germany	1951	Manufacture cement blocks, building 14 one-family units and 8 two-family units
Backnang, Germany	1952	Construction of 20 multifamily homes, 132 family dwellings
Greece (several proj.)	1952	Agricultural and community development
Wedel, Germany	1953	Construction of 12, 4 apartment houses
Chaco, Paraguay	1953	Trans-Chaco road projec
Jordan	1953	MCC programs, IVS-comm. devel.
Enkenbach, Germany	1953	Construction of 17 multifamily units
Kore	1953	Relief and community service
Peru	1954	LeTourneau Road building project and Le Tourneau Foundation educational work
Vienna, Austria	1955	Brethren/Mennonite renovation of Evangelical Church's Karlsschule, a Protestant School
Bechterdiessen, Gmy.	1955	Forty-five houses for 90 family units
Algeria	1955	Two projects of 30 small houses each, plus agricultural education and social work
Congo/Zaire	1955	Assist AIM, MCC relief and construction
Nepal	1956	Comm/village development, medical with United Mission to Nepal
Vietnam	1957	Relief, medical assistance, education, and agricultural development
Morocco	1958	Agricultural education, social work, construction (with Eirene)[27]
Salzburg, Austria	1961	Building 6 four-family refugee units and church for Apostolic Christian (Nazarene) group
Crete	1961	Agricultural demonstration/development and education
Israel	1961	Assisting MCC in refugee and development work
Bolivia	1961	Community/agricultural extension, indigenous resettlement
India	1961	Community/agricultural development
Burundi	1962	MCC material aid, mission leprosarium
Nigeria	1966	Agriculture, relief, construction
Haiti	1967	Assist MCC community development
Mexico	1967	Rural community/agricultural development
Brazil	1969	Community education/agricultural development

Sources: Urie Bender, *Soldiers of Compassion*; Robert Kreider and Rachel Waltner Goosen, *Hungry, Thirsty, a Stranger*; *Euro-Pax News*; *MCC Annual Reports*; MCC Files; miscellaneous documents and correspondence.

When this table is studied, it reveals that the Pax men were involved in an amazing range of cultures and a variety of projects and specialized activities. How did these projects materialize and how did they evolve and diversify?

Clearly the beginning of the Pax movement grew out of the crucial refugee emergency in Europe. In a larger sense, this diversity was rooted in the fact that Pax was a flexible arm of MCC, and MCC represented the Mennonite community's commitment to a world-wide relief and service ministry with needs that constantly exceeded resources. From an MCC headquarters administrative perspective, Pax suddenly provided an unexpected supply of manpower to fill some of these needs. An analysis of the nature of the projects and the locations bears this out.[28]

The Pax projects also demanded a wide cross-section of skills. While most of the Pax men did not have specialized training, they brought a wide range of general skills to the program. It is easy to deduce that the rural farm and village life that nurtured most of the fellows provided them with a broad range of experiences and abilities which, coupled with common sense and religious commitment, was a basic ingredient for their success.

This is already implied in the 1952 MCC Annual Report:

> We cannot take time here to relate all the experiences and accomplishments of the Pax Services Program in Europe and Jordan, but these young men, by their willingness and cheerfulness in carrying out their work assignments, have won their way into the hearts of the people with whom they are working and have built an enviable reputation for themselves.[29]

Furthermore, the laconic comment in the annual report of 1975 that the executive committee (endnote 39) had decided to no longer designate "Pax" when appointing these young suggests that the Pax spirit had so infused the program that it became a trait of the larger MCC structure.

From Relief to Development

A review of the types of projects Pax men conducted, (see Table 2) beginning with the project in Greece in 1952, reveals that many were essentially development projects. The majority of projects after 1955, beginning with Algeria, Nepal, and Morocco, can be classified as technical and organizational assistance aimed at helping communities become more self sufficient and independent. There is considerable variety in the definition of development, but one offered by Denis Goulet, compatible with Anabaptist beliefs, proposes that development include sustenance, self-esteem, and freedom from servitude.

> Sustenance includes having the basic needs of physical survival—food, health, housing and security. Self esteem refers to a sense of self worth, dignity, respect, and honor, and freedom is to be understood in the sense of emancipation from alienating material conditions of life and from social servitude to nature, ignorance, other people, misery, institutions, and dogmatic beliefs.[30]

These goals were evident in Pax's first development project in Greece. The full story of this project is still to be told, but the canning project, the agricultural crops, and community organization, all only part of what took place there, reflect Goulet's understanding of development. The same could be said of Pax work in Algeria, Bolivia, Congo, Haiti, and Mexico beginning in 1955 (randomly selected from Table 2).

This is not the place to expand the discussion of development beyond its relevance for the Pax story. It is important to note, however, that Pax was a pioneer effort in Mennonite development work and that this has not been generally recognized. In a survey of development work in the Mennonite community, Henry Rempel suggests that MCC was involved in development work in helping the Mennonite refugees become settled in South America. Strangely, he suggests that CPS camps were active in development work, and gives only one short paragraph to Pax, stating that

> in part motivated by the military draft in the United States, a program called Pax (peace) was set up for young American men to serve abroad, with specialized skills. Early programs included housing reconstruction in Europe and agricultural rehabilitation in Greece. Subsequently the program expanded to include road construction, and development

and vocational training projects in a number of low-income countries in Latin America and Africa.[31]

Rempel devotes the majority of the discussion on development to describing how Mennonite Economic Development Associates (MEDA) was formed in 1954, launching its first development work in Paraguay with subsequent work in many countries. Curiously, Rempel also devotes a long section to the development role that the Teachers Abroad Program (TAP) played, while Pax, receives only one paragraph.[32]

The theoretical and professional significance of Pax development work remains to be researched and analyzed. Its impact on the receiving communities has long been known, however, and is discussed in Chapter 7, as well as in *Soldiers of Compassion* and other sources. One further practical observation is that Pax men's experience in development work contributed to the launching of a number of professional careers in development. Among others, examples include Ken Graber and Calvin Miller in Bolivia, Arlin Hunsberger in Haiti, Dean Linsenmeyer in Mexico, Harold Miller and Fremont Regier in Africa, and Menno Wiebe in Canada.[33]

Chapter 6

Organization and Life of Pax

This book, a brief survey of the entire Pax program, cannot possibly convey the texture and the spirit of the Pax experience and unit life. Urie Bender's *Soldiers of Compassion* presents broader and deeper insight into Pax projects, including the backgrounds of selected Pax volunteers, personal accounts of their experiences, their inner life, and how they changed. The book also includes names of most of the men who served until 1969 as well as a list of all the countries where they served. *Soldiers* ends in 1968, seven years before the program officially closed in 1975.

A survey of sources makes it obvious that Pax men served in remote, even "romantic" and exotic places which had been unknown to them. Documentation of this aspect of the Pax experience awaits further publication of the diaries and memoirs of Pax men.[1] But little of the organizational structure, operation, life, and work of the Pax units has been included in Bender's book or elsewhere.

This chapter, then, primarily gives more information on the larger units. Even so, a comprehensive description cannot be provided. That task may never be completed, although segments of the units' experience have been reviewed and documented through reunions and in communications of specific groups of Pax men who served in the different projects.

The Pax Organization

The Pax organization was something of an anomalous entity in the MCC organization at the Akron headquarters. From the beginning, the Pax program was under the direction of the Executive Secretary of MCC.[2] The day-to-day responsibility for its administration, however, was delegated to the assistant executive secretary and then to the director of overseas relief services.

The actual administration of the Pax program depended on the nature of the various "theaters" in which the program operated. There was a European Pax director from the beginning of the program until the units in Europe were closed down, but the lines of responsibility were anything but simple and clear. For example, the first director actually reported to five different levels of offices.[3] (See Appendix D for a diagram from *Pax Handbook, 1952,* for the lines of authority.) Later versions of the *Handbook* provide detailed information on the policies regarding allowances, clothing, and vacations and conform closely to the policies in force for all MCC relief and service workers abroad.

The units in non-European locations such as Paraguay, Bangladesh, Africa, and various other countries were administered from Akron, usually through the Relief section with local country directors serving as directors in these locations. Typically the Pax men served in projects which were attached to an already existing local MCC program, and the men participated in the local MCC unit life. In fact, the specific work that the Pax unit performed was usually identified and arranged for by the MCC operations already in existence.

In many of the places where the men served, a Pax unit structure did not exist, since there were only one or two Pax assignees there. Pax men were also loaned to the EIRENE Morocco project and Milton Harder, an earlier MCC worker and later director of the MVS program in Europe became leader of that unit.[4] By September 1954, Pax men were loaned to the International Voluntary Work Camps Section of UNESCO in Paris. They included William Beitel, Paul Boyer, Paul Kissel, LaMarr Reichert, Rodney Penner, and Allen Schmidt. Kenneth Imhoff was sent to Egypt, Harold Neumann was assigned to Jordan, and Carl Jantzen went to Iraq.[5]

There were many projects that involved only one person or three to five people. These covered a wide spectrum of activities and normally consisted of "loaning" Pax men to a variety of jobs called "special assignments," some of which have already been described in earlier sections. The 1957 "MCC Annual Report" states that

> A number of Pax men are serving on special assignments. Two men are serving in the Pax administrative office, several are assisting in the MCC children's homes at Bad Duerkeim and at Valdoie, France, and near Brussels, Belgium. One man has been helping in the community center work at Kaiserslautern and one man at the Peace Center at Heerewegen, Holland.

For an example of the variety of assignments, see the experience of Wilbur Maust, cited in Appendix D.

In Europe, many of the projects were the expansion of projects in which Mennonite Voluntary Service had already laid the groundwork. Pax persons were often loaned to MVS projects, or vice versa. Because the two programs had evolved different policies, concerns such as vacation time, allowances, and other issues occasionally created problems.[6]

Pax Field Personnel and Responsibilities

Calvin Redekop was the first director of the European Pax program and served from January 1950 until December 20, 1952. Curtis Janzen, who had helped mobilize and lead the MVS program, was loaned from MVS to become the second director, serving during 1953. In 1954, Dwight Wiebe became European director and the Pax program expanded rapidly under his energetic and visionary leadership. Wiebe served until the end of 1957; Orville Schmidt served as Pax secretary at the Kaiserslautern, Germany office assisting Wiebe. Ray Kauffman became director in 1958 and served for a year. During this time, Jim Juhnke and Glen Good were Pax office assistants. In 1959 Robert Good became director and Juhnke continued to serve as an assistant.

One of the MCC Executive Committee's concerns in setting up Pax units was the social and spiritual welfare of the young men. In his instructions to A. Lloyd Swartzentruber the first Pax pastor, William Snyder, MCC assistant executive secretary, wrote, "As Unit Leader of these 19 men, you will be responsible for them both on and off their project. We ask that you devote considerable time to counseling the men as they may have need of your pastoral help."[7] A bit later he added, "It would be quite unrealistic to think that we will not have problems of some nature with the Pax Unit I. We trust the Lord will lead you in anticipating such problems and in meeting them for the benefit of all concerned."[8]

I concluded that one reason Akron headquarters hesitated to encourage more cooperation and integration with the European MVS program is that they feared the men were too young and inexperienced to handle the challenges and temptations in such a setting. In fact, the second Pax pastor, Jesse Short, stated in a letter to O. O. Miller, H. A. Fast, H. S. Bender, and Cal Redekop that mixing MVS people with Paxers was not a good idea.

Noting this concern, Swartzentruber took his work seriously and sent Snyder a "grade sheet" listing the "boys" with categories for place of work, attitude, quality of work, and participation in unit life. He gave a range of grades from good to very good and no one got a grade of poor. Snyder apparently did not expect such a detailed and "academic" report, for he somewhat playfully responded,

> I suppose we should know you better, Brother Swartzen-truber, in [our] trying to evaluate what 'good' and 'very good' means. Some teachers in school are very hard graders and a 'B' from such a teacher is worth an 'A' from certain others. [However] I think you are fair-minded and we will accept your grading (system) of the young men without discounting any of the grades.[9]

Swartzentruber and his wife, Mary, lived at the Niedebieber [Neuwied] unit and periodically visited the men at the Espelkamp unit. Swartzentruber assumed his responsibility included interpreting the work of the Pax program to local religious and government leaders when invited to do so, and helping the men become involved in local Mennonite religious activities. This format was continued by the Pax pastors who followed Swartzentruber.

Mary Swartzentruber, who joined her husband several months after the first unit arrived, served as Pax matron, a role that developed in all the later projects. Mary served as cook, seamstress, general housekeeper, and "Mom" away from home to all the boys. Immediately upon the arrival of Pax Unit I, Swartzentruber realized that a "mother" should be part of the unit and requested that his wife be allowed to join the unit. He wrote:

> In reference to my wife coming here to help with the work, I feel that it will be a very great help, not only from the angle of the cooking, but also in the laundering. John [one of the Pax fellows] just now came from the laundry and said he paid 8.70 DM for a little laundry for the five of us. We did not have nearly all of our things in, and this only half of our boys. There will be another laundry bill next week. Brother Graber advised me to buy a machine and do the washing at our home.[10]

A. Lloyd and Mary served the Pax units at Neuwied and Espelkamp from April 1951 until summer of 1952. The Pax pastor and matron roles, so well modeled by "Pop and Mom" as they were affectionately called, continued in the European theater of Pax operations. Pax pastor Jesse Short and his wife, who served as matron, lived at Backnang and served the Pax units from 1952 until 1953. John and Katie Shenk served 1953-1954. In 1954, D.C. Kauffman became Pax pastor, succeeded by J. P. Duerksen for a term from 1955 to 1957. Noah Good shepherded the Pax men in 1958, and from 1959 to 1961, Clarence Hiebert was in charge of spiritual nurture.

The Pax pastors were responsible for the spiritual and emotional welfare of the Pax men, but the unit "Pop and Mom" roles were performed for the entire period of the construction phase by Erika and Kurt Klaassen, who lived in a reconstructed barracks next door just like the Pax men. Erika served as mother/cook and Kurt as father and general parent.

The two were beloved by all the Pax men and have maintained many relationships to the present. After a visit by a Pax group in 1995, Kurt and Erika wrote, "These hours with you were so meaningful and invigorating for all of us [here at Espelkamp], that it took us some days to recover enough to resume our normal routine."[11]

Changing Activities and Personnel Responsibilities

Dispersing Pax members and units to other parts of Europe and Africa, and later to other parts of the world made the role of Pax unit leaders/pastor/matron along the European model less workable. To bridge the gap, some of the Pax unit's functions and structures were taken over by the MCC personnel in areas where Pax members served.

In other countries where only one or a few Pax men were stationed, leadership and spiritual nurture were tailored to the situation. Both the Bolivian Pax unit (described in Chapter 5) and the Paraguay project illustrate this. When feasible the Pax men there attended Mennonite church services in Asuncion or in the colonies. Harry Harder and his wife served as resident parents with Harry, the project and unit leader, and his wife serving as unit matron.[12]

The matron role continued in some form in almost all the larger units and expanded to perform a significant function. Duties not only included the oversight of the food preparation, laundry, and mending of clothes, but planning for social activities, community relations, vacation travel, and the like. The matron become the morale booster, maintaining a "feminine" milieu in the face of "degenerating" tendencies among fellows just recently separated from the influence of their mothers. In short, a matron was a mix of housekeeper, cook, surrogate mother, and female presence.

Evaluating the role that "Mutti" played at Karlsschule, one Pax man wrote that

> We feel that a matron plays a major role in the unit spirit of our Pax life. In fact, we are tempted to say that the positive contributions which a matron makes to the unit living are even more important than the physical contributions such as cooking, housekeeping, etc.[13]

In another testimony to the positive feelings matrons created, one Pax fellow wrote a letter to a matron inviting her to the 50 year celebration in 2001:

> Dear Hannelora: I will not put off [writing] any longer. [Many] times I have paused and in my memory, have reminisced and gone over old memories. Almost 45 years ago,

when Dwight Wiebe, Robert Schrag, Arlo Kasper, LaMar Kopp, Lois Kramer, Ilse Franz and I were in Kaiserslautern, you were our wonderful matron, our wonderful cook, and a wonderful human being. The Pax fellows have not forgotten you. In 1998 there was a Pax reunion at Miracle Camp in Michigan. There were quite a number of Pax fellows there from Backnang and they all remembered you very fondly.[14]

A brief reference to the Matron's role appeared in the November 1955 issue of the *Euro Pax News*. Under the caption "Matrons Play a Vital Role," the editor writes,

> One of the reasons that Germany [sic] I-W's are not merely building crews is the fact that each unit has a matron. Not just cooks and housekeepers, these American and Canadian ladies contribute greatly to general unit life, help in contacting the new settlers and continually do their utmost to make attractive 'homes away from home' for the I-Ws.

Wives of unit directors often served in that capacity as well.

Matrons who served in Germany, Greece, and Austria include Elsie Bechtel, Hannelora Bergen, Tina Warkentin Bohn, Lena Bontrager, Irma Bowman, Ann Driedger, Evelyn Ediger, Mrs. Elbert Esau, Anna Ewert, Isabel Gingerich, Catharine Miller Hartzler, Beulah Heisey, Fokje Hendricks, Erika Klaassen, Susan Krahn, Lois Martin, Margaret Martin, Nettie Redekop Baer, Emma Schlichting, Mrs. Jesse Short, Fannie Schrock, Katie Shenk, Susan Willms, Lena Swartentruber, and Orpha Zimmerly.[15]

Matron status was by no means uniform, and the role was performed in a variety of ways, depending on the matron and the nature, size, and structure of the unit. In some cases where the age differences between the fellows and matrons were not that great, romantic impulses were not totally absent. In the smaller units, and in non-European contexts such as Bolivia, Paraguay, and the Congo, the matron role was performed in a variety of ways.

The matron's role was not the only one dictated by unit size and circumstances. With larger projects, the units were headed by a unit director/leader, usually the oldest or most mature member of the Pax unit. In the early years, Mennonite

Voluntary Service (MVS) workers who had been active in the area with considerable experience would be asked to be unit leaders.[16] This was the case at Espelkamp where the Pax unit was directed by a resident MCC/MVS person, beginning with Menno Gaeddert. Gaeddert had served at Espelkamp since January 1950 and was appointed unit leader from April 1951 until December 1952. Similarly, Ivan Holdeman was the unit leader in Greece from 1952-1954 followed by Larry Eisenbeis.

In the non-European sectors, the area MCC director often was a field coordinator for the Pax projects, while a member of the Pax team was usually appointed as project leader. Overall, however, direction remained in the Akron, Pennsylvania office. There, most of the personnel and financial aspects were managed by the director of overseas relief, while administrative decisions were made by the MCC Executive Office. The Bolivian program, for example, reflects this pattern.

Each Pax project had its own significant history, objectives, charm, and even romance. The Pax unit in the Paraguayan Chaco, which has been documented and preserved in Gerhard Ratzlaff's *Die Ruta Transchaco* includes all of these features. The road finally got underway at the end of February 1957, when after years of discussion, disappointments and false starts, the Paraguayan government, the International Cooperation Administration (ICA), and MCC, signed documents to begin the construction. The services of up to fifteen Pax men undoubtedly helped to make the project a joint Mennonite and Paraguayan government endeavor.

The structure of the Paraguay unit was described by Eddie Ratzlaff, who arrived in Paraguay on December 21, 1954, to work on the road building project: "The machinery we needed for the Trans-Chaco project was delayed in customs so we worked on inter-colony roads and other MCC and colony projects." Living in Filadelfia, Chaco, during the interim period, Ratzlaff reported,

> I worked with Bob Unruh, [also] breaking sod with the MCC tractor and then at KM 81 with Dr. John Schmidt. Bob and Myrtle Unruh were the leaders of our unit of five Pax men. We had a number of North American leaders visit us who gave us encouragement."[17]

From every perspective, the Pax men made a remarkable contribution to the completion of the road, consisting of 398 kilometers of road through difficult terrain and climate. It still serves as the basic lifeline between the Mennonite colonies and Asuncion.

Ratzlaff presents the personal accounts of some of the fellows who served on that project, namely Menno Wiebe, Clair Brenneman, Robert Ediger, John Huebert, Virgil Claassen, Daniel Keith Yoder, and Leslie Nafziger. MCC leader Harry Harder was director of the project and Chaco Mennonites also provided volunteers. The road work, conducted under the Paraguayan government's supervision, was similar to the convoluted relationships of the European Pax projects.

One almost "fictional thriller" indicates the range of experiences the men had. Once Menno Wiebe was arrested in Asuncion on the assumption he was spying. Wiebe aroused suspicions by wearing a red shirt and taking pictures during the "Dia de la Asuncion" (Day of the Ascension), which included a parade with some of the machines the Pax fellows were using to build the Trans-Chaco road. Wiebe was jailed incognito, without passport. During his arrest Wiebe signaled one of the other Pax men, motioning that he did not have his passport. Later, the Pax man smuggled the passport into the jail cell.

Wiebe was subjected to some rather hostile interrogations and spent a very uncomfortable night in jail. However, his dependable Pax buddies sneaked some blankets and some food to him. It took considerable negotiating on the part of the MCC Paraguayan director Frank Wiens, who called the American and British Consulates before Wiebe was finally released late the following day.[18]

Domestic Life in the Units

Most units undoubtedly experienced their own versions of unforgettable events, along with the humdrum of everyday work, that approached boredom in some cases. But every unit developed traditions that symbolized its life together. For example, "horse and goggle," a procedure used to democratically determine who got the extra piece of pie, was religiously practiced in the German units. Each unit, especially the larger ones, also included "characters" who enlivened the atmosphere with their antics and humor.

In his diary, Peter Neufeld notes, "Today, (September 6) 5 new boys came and joined the unit (at Espelkamp) In this group was a —————— who for some reasons unknown had the nickname Sparkey (not his real nickname)."[19] That day a member of the Executive Committee of MCC, Henry Fast, who at the time was the European MCC director stationed in Basel, Switzerland; C. L Graber; General Lewis B. Hershey, director of Selective Service; and several other MCC leaders were visiting the Pax units.

After a hearty lunch, the dignitaries expressed their appreciation and congratulations to the Pax men for the fine work they were doing. This was followed by congenial expressions of farewell and handshaking, along with the normal profuse picture taking which was endemic among Pax men. Sparkey[20] casually asked the visiting officials to kindly line up close together so Paxers could take a group picture. Of course they gladly obliged. As a number of other Pax photographers gathered to focus their cameras, Sparkey crowded into the middle of the group of photographers, moved in closer, aimed his camera straight at General Hershey, and pressed the shutter. At that moment the General received a healthy squirt of water in his left eye.

Stunned silence followed with embarrassment and consternation on the faces of both the dignitaries and the Pax men. But Hershey was the first to recover from the shock. Quickly realizing the humor of the event he began to chuckle, then to laugh with abandon, and was soon joined by MCC officials.

Several Pax men, who had been informed of Sparkey's intended stunt, had remained back in the bunkhouse, too embarrassed to observe the event. The dignitaries headed for the MCC vehicle, still laughing as they got into the car and left to inspect other important MCC projects. There was little productive work at the Espelkamp work site for the remainder of the day.[21] Neufeld concludes, "Sparkey was no respecter of persons. They all got it, even Gen. Hershey." Neufeld concludes the day's events in his diary by noting that "Gen. Hershey did approve this service later."[22]

Many "off time" activities also enriched and expanded the life of the Pax men and the communities in which they served—"busier than college days," according to one Pax fellow.[23] In Germany, for example, "A look into unit schedules reveals a part of the busy Pax life. Each unit wants to feel itself a church and arranges for regular devotional activities. Weekly Bible study periods, prayer meetings, and Sunday school hours are held with the men alternating as leaders."[24]

Other activities in the larger German/Austrian units included Pax choirs, which sang for enjoyment in the units themselves and in local community events. In Enkenbach, Sam Dietzel directed a Mennonite church youth choir that included several Pax men. "An eighteen-member chorus traveled to Berlin, singing at refugee camps, a large prison, and the Mennonite Church in the city. An octet, organized later, also traveled to Berlin, singing for refugees in various camps."[25]

Social gatherings with area youth groups and Bible studies for local children often involved Paxers. Garber states that the Karlsschule "fellows became members of choirs, leaders in prayer services, teachers in Sunday schools, directors of youth groups, and in general, did an outstanding job of leavening the Protestant lump in Catholic Austria."[26]

Unit recreation included baseball teams and other games, and there were occasional competitions with local community youth groups. During the 1960s, there were also musical groups that performed at a variety of events. In 1962, a Pax quartet was organized and sang in Mennonite churches in Europe and the United States.

Situated in the heart of Europe, the early Pax units traveled extensively during their two weeks of vacation each year and managed to obtain a rather comprehensive perspective on Europe. They often went in small groups and traveled in a rented car or by train. But Pax men also organized major tours to Palestine beginning in 1955 and continuing every year until 1960. Orville Schmidt notes, "Charles Yoder was the midwife of the first tour and that must have been just simply one heck of a birth process. When you stop to think about it, what a vacation. It's like Bob said in his piece on Wiebe: 'we all expected to travel, but Athens, Jerusalem, Cairo?' "[27]

One indication of the vigor and strength of the European Pax program was the *Euro Pax News* established in September 1954. This quarterly journal informed the Pax units about each others' activities, built morale, and notified people back home as to what was happening in Europe in Pax. Robert Schrag was the first editor and continued until July 1956. Arlo Kasper was editor from October 1956 to August 1957. James Eigsti was editor for several issues in 1958, followed by Gerald Bender, who edited the paper until it was discontinued in May 1959 with volume 6, no. 2.[28]

The Pax units conducted an annual retreat that was significant for the Pax men. As Paul Hershberger states,

> Another unique Pax extracurricular was the annual Pax conference. This was set up on a two- or three-day schedule at some central point. The sessions offered inspirational messages, practical how-to talks, and plenty of time to learn to know each other. The conference days also provided a convenient context in which to air gripes, makes suggestions, and arrange job transfers.[29]

The Pax units' most ambitious activities were the "Pax Peace Conferences." The first was held at Schloss Leopoldstein, near Eisenerz, Austria, March 11-16, 1959. Moderated by Pax director Ray Kauffman, the program featured Andre Trocme, Peter Dyck, Clarence Bauman, and Erwin Goering, and music included the Enkenbach Quartet.

The program's "Introduction" proclaims, "All Christians agree that peace is the will of God. MCC Pax men go at least one step further. We claim war is contrary to the will of God, and consequently Christians are obliged not to become a part of the military machine. We think of our neighbor as the community of mankind—a world-wide brotherhood." One highlight was Andre Trocme's speech, entitled "Christian Responsibility in Areas of International Tension." Meanwhile Gerald Bender wrote a "Summary of Findings."

Smaller Pax units often integrated their activities with the MCC unit, or the sponsoring agency to which they were attached. In situations where only one or two Pax men were stationed, the Paxers were responsible for their own inner life and social activities. This was the case for the Iraq unit in which Carl R. Jantzen served. He volunteered for Pax service in Germany in1953. "But when William Snyder told me about the proposed work in Iraq I did not hesitate long in consenting to go if I could be of use." He was assigned to Germany first (about four months), but then was assigned (the MCC word was "seconded") to go to Iraq under International Voluntary Service.[30] The IVS team was

> composed partly of trained personnel—agriculturists, public health nurse, and home economist for instance—and partly of generalists, one might say, usually with a rural background. The first team director was Eldon Burke, a member of the Church of the Brethren. Our job was to work with the Iraq (sic) government in building up a demonstration farm and training center in village development work.[31]

The Integration of PAX and MVS Activities

Mennonite Voluntary Service workers were often involved in Pax projects and unit activities; and conversely, many Pax men were assigned to MVS projects. MVS units often prepared the living quarters for the coming Pax units, not only in Espelkamp but also in Vienna, Austria; Backnang, Germany; and Witmarsum, Holland.

In these and other locations, MVS served as the cooperative link with the Mennonites of the French, German, Dutch, and Swiss conferences. Many young people from these sending Mennonite congregations became part of the volunteer program and connected their congregations to American members of the faith. In many other projects, such as the Witmarsum Mennonite Church, Krefeld church restoration, and smaller projects, MVS provided the initial leadership and preparations for the specific work itself as well as the framework for inducting and integrating volunteers from the European Mennonite churches into the projects.[32]

Pax men were loaned to MVS projects for many years. Richard Rush, member of Pax Unit #1, remembers that

> Shortly before my term in Pax was over (Espelkamp and Neuwied), Al Roupp and I were asked to join the Mennonite Voluntary Service unit. The task at hand was to help

build a church at Zeilsheim, near Frankfurt. This was a new community of resettled refugees (including Mennonites). Our group had American, German, Canadian, and Dutch volunteers in it.[33]

Rush finished his work at Zeilsheim and his MVS unit was transferred to Windischgarsten, Austria, where "A Brethren service summer camp had been helping to build a church, and after they left we went in to help their struggling congregation realize their dream of having their own church building." After completing the project, Rush was sent to Lubbeck for several weeks, and then to help with a summer work camp at Hohenlimburg.

> After a few days there I got a cable from Cal Redekop telling me to go to Gronau. Dwight Swartzentruber was returning home and since Gronau would soon close no new workers would be sent there. I was to work there until October 1952, when I would return home.[34]

The Progression of Pax

This integration of North American Pax men with indigenous Mennonite and other volunteers linked specific congregations with Mennonite institutions, places, and peoples of other congregations in many countries, especially in Europe but also around the world. Mennonite ecumenicity was nurtured in an unprecedented manner through this process, similar to MCC's functions in the United States and Canada. Near the high point of the Pax program in terms of persons serving in Pax, and the number of projects being conducted, a 1962 MCC press release stated that

> In 1961 the Mennonite Central Committee Pax program completed its first 10 years of service. During this decade, Pax has expanded from a program of housing construction for refugees in Germany to one giving varied services in other areas of Europe and in Asia, Africa, and South America. With the increasing prosperity of Western Europe, the Pax program is now shifting its emphasis to areas of greater need, particularly in Asia. Plans for 1962 call for an increase in the number of Paxmen need in the Far East. In these projects around the world, the Pax program aims to offer op-

portunities for service abroad to young men with a variety of talents and skills. The Pax ideals continue to be the expression of Christian love through hard work and the building of peace through understanding.

MCC releases regarding Pax expanded, and Pax assignments regularly appeared in the annual MCC reports and personnel listings. News releases were frequently printed in the Mennonite denominational papers, and Mennonite colleges began to see the significance of Pax for their educational purposes. In 1967, a "College Credit for Service" brochure with the word *PAX* in psychedelic colors was released by the Council of Mennonite Colleges (CMC). This pamphlet announced college credit for Pax appointees who were heading for the rapidly expanding work in Africa.

In 1963, Pax men were working in Algeria, Burundi, Congo, and Kenya. The brochure stated the program would be extended to Latin America in 1968. No statistical information is available on the extent of student enrollment in the program. It is clear the Pax movement was increasingly recognized and respected. By 1961, Pax had become established, and possibly even institutionalized in the larger MCC program, but its growth and success may also have contributed to the loss of its identity. After 1963, MCC annual reports no longer listed Pax in a separate section. In fact, the *MCC Annual Report* for 1963 reads,

> At one time in Europe it almost appeared if Pax were a separate organization from MCC. The Pax office was not located in the same building or city as the MCC office. Pax had its own director, its own budget, vehicles, and publication. This has gradually and noticeably changed. Today the Pax office is incorporated into the MCC office, at Frankfurt, there is no Pax director, no separate Pax vehicles, no separate publications, and beginning with fiscal year 1964, there will be no separate Pax budget.[35]

No reasons were given for this change, but it is probable that MCC desired to integrate the Pax program into existing projects. It may also be that the Pax directors in Europe were promoting Pax so aggressively that MCC headquarters increasingly feared losing control of the program. MCC's uneasiness over too close a collaboration with MVS may have helped to limit the program.

In addition, the draft was terminated in December 1972, and the refugee housing problem was basically alleviated by 1960. Since Pax had been seen as a solution for both, this may be why the Pax program was phased out in 1975. The times and the urgencies of that time obviously had changed. But does this fully resolve the demise of Pax? (See Appendix C for aims of Pax.)

Although Pax's pioneer development work in Greece and Crete became a major form of MCC work abroad, it could be maintained that the original European idea of Pax was not compatible with the ongoing goals of MCC. An international service organization bringing young people from a variety of backgrounds and lifestyles working for peace and betterment was not the way MCC customarily operated. The idealism of post-World War II volunteerism in the name of peace, helping to undo the devastation and destruction of war, may have receded, both in the minds of the Pax volunteers and of MCC as conditions improved. Other concerns took center stage, such as the emerging nations in Africa, which were viewed as needing help to become self-sustaining.

(above) Peru Pax builders, with C. N. Hostetter, chairman, MCC; and R. G. LeTourneau in foreground. MCC-AMC

(below) Clair Brenneman in the back machine running a "Tournapull" and two Chaco Mennonites volunteers in front machine on the Trans-Chaco road project, 1953-1973. MCC-AMC

Dan Roth assisting the business manager of Pusan Korea Children's home, 1961. MCC-AMC

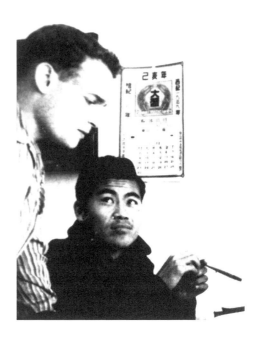

Daryl Mast directing construction of rice storage bin, Bangladesh, 1975. MCC-AMC

Chapter 7

The Meaning of Pax

The Pax men's "voluntary service interlude" in forty-plus foreign lands and cultures primarily and fundamentally contributed to their intellectual, psychological, and spiritual growth. As one fellow states in the research conducted by Larry Kehler, "Pax was a wonderful eye-opener for me and gave knowledge and a view of conditions in this world for which I am very thankful. I just praise God for giving me this precious experience. I only regret that I did not make more of the once-in-a-lifetime opportunity which I had (Germany, 1958-1960)."[1]

Misfortunes and Tragedies along the Way

But the success of the Pax story was tempered with accidents and tragedies. Several men had to be sent home because they could not manage the separation from family and home, were unable to function in the frontier-type atmosphere, or failed to make the necessary cultural adjustments in a strange new environment.

Two men, Simon and Eli Miller, drowned in Greece in a swimming accident in June 1954. This shocked and saddened the unit as well as the community. Leon Yoder, who served in Indonesia from 1962, contracted cancer and died after returning home. Carl Kauffman first assigned to Hong Kong, was later transferred to Vietnam. He served there until September 1, 1967, and was killed in a motorcycle accident in Singapore on September 16, 1967, during a tour after his service term ended.

One of the most painful accidents took place in the Congo in 1958, when Larry Kauffman, with a fellow Paxer, a Mennonite missionary and his two sons, and several local natives, took a three-day trip on the Kasai river. Larry disappeared as the party was landing on an island in the river to camp for the night. To this day no one knows exactly how it happened, but Fremont Regier writes that

> on the point of the sand bar around which we were maneuvering the dugout, sand went out into the river and the river was running over it and in the process was depositing sand, like over a cliff, then dropping off sharply on the downstream side of the 'bar. I think maybe Larry stepped off the edge of the just-under-water downside bar and was suddenly in deep water with pretty strong current (as he was trying to bring the boat to a landing spot). Larry never shouted, called, or said anything at all that any of us heard. There are crocodiles and hippos in the Kasai, and it is possible that a crock did get him and pull him under, but no one knows.[2]

A near-tragedy encountered in the line of duty involved Gene Bergman and Jon Snyder. The two were stationed at Stanleyville, Congo, as support staff for the new university being established there. In 1964, the threat of civil chaos and war increased, but both Bergman and Snyder opted to remain with Mel Loewens (the rector at the University of Kinshasa).

On November 24, 1964, Bergman, Snyder, and a group of white missionaries were held hostage by the Simbas and threatened with execution. "Seeing them (the whites) scatter, the *Simbas* again opened fire in all directions. Larson, Snyder, and Davis vaulted over thee wall, broke down the door and took refuge inside."[3] The Belgian paratroopers who had surrounded the city managed to save most of the hostages, including Bergman and Snyder.

The only Pax casualty occurring in the line of duty took place in Vietnam. Because of the country's increasing refugee needs, in 1954 MCC opened a program in the central highlands, distributing relief supplies as well as assisting in the operation of a hospital and clinic. In 1956 Pax men were seconded to a hospital building project of the Christian and Missionary Alliance, one of the few Protestant groups still operating in Vietnam in the 1950s. Ultimately, MCC developed a program which involved 117 persons and the agency did not leave Vietnam until 1975.

MCC had been one of the few American organizations allowed in Vietnam during the U.S. military adventure there. The heightening crisis of the Vietnam war affected MCC as well, for there was intense debate in Mennonite constituencies whether MCC had any business in Vietnam. But this program was probably the closest that MCC and Pax ever got to the quagmire of actual hostilities. The irony and agony of these events has not yet been fully digested by the Mennonite community. (For an intense analysis of the struggle, see Earl Martin's book, *Reaching the Other Side*.)

In May 1962, Daniel Gerber was abducted by the Viet Cong from the grounds of the Banmethout Leprosarium, where he was serving. In his application to serve as a Pax volunteer in Vietnam, Gerber had written, "Christ taught love and that is what his children must do."[4]

Gerber's fiancé witnessed the abduction but escaped. She returned to the States and provided his parents with the firsthand account of the abduction, sharing her commitment to return to Vietnam to serve where she and Daniel had worked together. Soon after her return, she was captured and killed by the Viet Cong. No trace of Gerber has ever been found, and there is no closure to his disappearance. Pax fellows remained to serve in Vietnam until the MCC program was shut down in 1975. The last U.S. ground troops had left Vietnam in August 11, 1972, with a ceasefire signed in Paris, January 27, 1973.

When the United States withdrew from the war in Vietnam, the military draft became unnecessary. The U.S. government terminated the military draft In December 1972, and announced the decision on January 27, 1973. The military solution to economic and ideological conflicts had proven to be a colossal failure. The futility was symbolized by the murder of 47,321 young men and the ongoing suffering of both American and Vietnamese survivors. The massive peace demonstrations and protests of the late 1960s accentuated and memorialized the tragedy of the United States first major defeat in war and heightened the symbolic victory of the Pax idea, which had quietly worked at reducing human need and misery.

Pax Contributions to the Church

It is difficult to evaluate the impact of Pax. The program's philosophy of humble service and its Anabaptist emphasis on humility led to an unconcern about preserving a coherent record of the exact number of men who served, where they served, and the nature and amount of assistance they provided. So an accurate or exact statistical summary will probably never be produced.

This reflects the idealistic and non-bureaucratic nature of the program's vision and operations, which was to "get the job done." The official number and names of Pax men who served has not yet been definitively compiled but best available tabulations (See Table 1) indicate that 1,180 men served in the program, amounting to at least 2,360 man years.[5]

But the desire to make a positive contribution to the larger world, and to be more relevant is clearly expressed in both official records and personal accounts. The MCC Executive Committee's proposal authorizing Pax reads, "It was agreed that further effort should be made to open to our young men opportunities for civilian service of the greatest possible significance and relevance to human need and suffering resulting from modern warfare."[6]

The *1952 Pax Handbook* states that "as the progress of Pax Services is being developed and carried on we have set forth several aims." Point three noted, "It is our aim and hope that the total impact will help to promote international goodwill and understanding as we work together with citizens of other countries in a spirit of sharing and brotherly love."[7]

Did Pax make any impact on the world? This question was never critically studied from the Mennonite and MCC perspective. But from time to time MCC did evaluate the program, occasionally sending a church leader such as Harry Martens to investigate.

A more focused review took place in 1957, when the Executive Committee "request [ed] the administrative office to make a careful study of the future Pax program, including program and policies, and bring that report to the Executive Committee for consideration and possible action."[8] William T. Snyder and Robert Miller did the research and submitted their conclusions to the Executive Committee on December 14, 1957. Among other information they reported that

> We do not have information on the amount of personal support contributed by groups [that] arrange directly for their support. But a recent check indicated that a total of 79 men were contributing an average of $27.03 per month each toward their own support.[9]

The report's general conclusions stated that "The Pax program has been making a unique and valuable contribution in the relief and mission outreach. Our churches and our young men continue to have a strong interest in this service and new opportunities for service should be sought."[10] The five conclusions (presented in Appendix F) imply that the Pax men were most effective in rather strongly supervised contexts.

A skeptic or cynic might conclude that Pax operated between the Korean and Vietnam wars to keep the Mennonite young men out of the war. But this is also a favorable impact since close to 1,200 young men did not serve in futile, brutal, and even immoral war, especially the Vietnam war. This, in itself, is a positive contribution to the peace of the world, is a classic Mennonite stance used to defend the pacifist position. In essence, Mennonties believe that not contributing to the destructiveness of war, regardless of the geo-politics justifying war, is considered to be a positive contribution to peace.

Pax efforts did help specific people with specific needs, but in terms of affecting the Mennonite church's impact on the larger world, the question cannot be answered. There are no objective or universal measures by which this question can even be addressed. How could living with and helping a few Greek farmers rehabilitate their farms make any difference in history?

The Meaning of Pax for the Volunteers

We now turn to a review of what the Pax experience meant to the Pax men. It is much easier to investigate the impact that Pax made on individuals: here there is rather overwhelming and unequivocal evidence. *Soldiers of Compassion,* commissioned by MCC and researched and written by Urie Bender, is the best early source for information on how Pax affected the volunteers themselves and the impact they had on the recipients and communities at the various projects.

Further, families living in homes constructed by the Pax boys in the first Pax project had a concrete reason for appreciating the Paxers. "They build [houses] for us with their hands, [but] they also build by their example—They serve God."[11]

At the project in Vienna several years later, a Viennese newspaper commented that the Pax boys' contribution "serves the cause of peace. While their fellow Americans in uniform had to leave Austria ninety days after the State Treaty was signed, they, wearing work clothes, stayed in Vienna, [not with] helmet, rifle or bayonet, but with trowel, shovel and gauge."[12] A Greek Orthodox priest, speaking for the farmers in northern Greece, said that "We remember your various and vivid Christian examples. You are the great benefactors of our village. . . . We assure you that your names will remain ineffaceable in our memory and that it will pass to the next generation."[13] The testimonials from recipients in later projects around the globe continue ad infinitum—Pax service was meaningful and appreciated.

The Pax experience also had a lifelong impact on participants. Most Pax men had completed a high school education; few had taken college classes. Unfortunately no information has become available indicating the educational level of the volunteers, but by inference we can obtain a little impression from a 1966 study entitled, "A Profile of Mennonite Personnel Involved in International Experience." In this important research Larry Kehler included a special focus on the Pax program. He states,

> Most of the Paxmen felt a strong urge to continue their education once they returned home. Fifty-nine (70 percent of a random sample of 86 persons) went back to school once their overseas assignment was completed. Twenty-six enrolled in college, twenty others completed their college work and then went on to graduate school, six went right into graduate school, four enrolled in trade schools, two went to Bible school, and one completed his high school and then enrolled in college. Thirty-six (42 percent) of the returned Paxmen earned B.A. or B.S. degrees after completion of their service abroad. Twenty-two percent (19) have

completed or are in the process of concluding work on a graduate degree.[14]

Almost every Pax man agrees that the two or more years of Pax service were the "most important years of our lives." Almost without exception, this service expanded the horizons of vision and possibilities.

One of the most common conclusions the Pax men stated about their experience was that it had been the most significant life-changing and future-determining experience of their lives.[15] One fellow typifies the universal response. Upon returning from his term of service in Paraguay, he stated,

> Pax changed my life. Even though I had one year of college before leaving, I was a pretty naive, provincial guy. Although I rebelled against some elements of it, I was still very much a part of my home community. When I started service, I suddenly became aware that world culture did not find its center in [his home community]. Pax service put me on a long road. But an interesting road on which I see unselfish sharing as the essential element. One on which I see Christ as having already walked.[16]

Another, having served nearly three years emphasized that "Pax was good to me. During the years as a Paxer, I grew up. I learned to slow my pace, to be more concerned about people than with things. I think I became more tolerant both of myself, in the tension between idealism and reality, and of others. Pax is a valid idea. It offers a service that is down to earth and relevant."[17] Paxers almost universally agreed, no doubt with some homage to humility, that "we benefited much more than the ones we served."

One of the best indicators of the depth and meaning of the Pax experience is the relationships that have persisted through the years. There is no objective source of data on the personal ties and relationships that were created in Pax and which survive to this day. But the reunions that have taken place on a relatively consistent basis in the United States and Canada are a rich source of subjective data. For example, the original group of twenty fellows and a second group have held numerous reunions. Another group, composed mainly of people from the Backnang and Enkenbach epoch, has established a strong tradition of sharing and bonding at a campground in Michigan. The Greece Pax men have sponsored numerous reunions and conducted trips to the Greek communities where they served.

The strength of this continuing bond was celebrated at the "Pax summit," publicized as a "Nationwide Pax Conference" and held at Camp Freidenswald on August 25-27, 1961. The *Gospel Herald* reported, "About 140 persons gathered for a nationwide Pax conference. Representation was made up largely of men who had served in the European area, although the conference was open to Pax men who had served in other areas as well. The conference program was planned to be both informational and inspirational."[18]

Among interesting events the *Gospel Herald* reported was the presence of "Demetrious Xouris, a student from Greece who attended Bethel College last year under the sponsorship of Pax men." The Bienenberg choir from Switzerland "highlighted the Saturday afternoon session." An indication of the caliber of the meeting, a panel discussion on "Possible Solutions to the Pax Men's Dilemma" was held in the evening moderated by Erwin Goering, former director of European Mennonite Voluntary Service, Dr. Paul Peachey, Dr. J. Winfield Fretz, and former Pax men Orville Schmidt and Jerry Bender.[19]

Despite these testimonials, the broad and profound ramifications of such a dislocating event can only be imagined. Coming from basically rural and traditional Mennonite communities, these men were quickly thrust into strange and challenging circumstances.

In the later years of the Pax program, some volunteers already had some college education, but in the beginning, few had finished high school and were relatively uniformed on world affairs. As the Kehler study indicates, however, many Pax men continued their post-Pax educations and changed their careers to embrace roles as pastors, teachers, and other service workers. This seems to be the best supporting argument that Pax was indeed a significant event for these men.

Numerous testimonies to the values of voluntary service have been offered within the Anabaptist context. And we must be reminded that Pax is but one sector in the history of volun-

teering for others. One attempt to evaluate the meaningful-
ness of voluntary service, including Pax, was an article written by Harry Martens who dedicated most of his life to a variety of church missions. Martens concludes his article by quot-
ing a refugee in Backnang, Germany:

> The work of the Pax men here in the Backnang settlement
> has become a concept—a symbol of Christian brotherly
> love and readiness to help. It certainly wasn't that way
> when the first members of Mennonite Voluntary Service ar-
> rived here. Nor was it that way when the first Pax men
> came to Backnang. Instead people seemed quite skeptical.
> People could not conceive that in this materialistic age,
> such strong Christian faith and so much idealism existed. I
> have never seen public opinion influenced as it has been
> by this undertaking.[20]

What was the driving force that caused these Pax men to
leave their protected communities and volunteer to give their
best energies and gifts for others? Only the Pax men themselves will know what sacrifices and dogged slogging day in
and day out were required on the varied projects. Were these
men romantic idealists? Were they trying to maximize the positive aspects of the draft by hoping to see a bit of the world?
This motive was not operative for the 110 Canadians who volunteered but who were not susceptible to being drafted.[21] But
the desire to travel and see a bit of the larger world beyond
their restricted communities was undoubtedly a part of the
motivation.[22]

Once on assignment, were the boys convinced that they
could do some good work with their own lives? Were they dis-
couraged at times, pessimistic about what could be done? The
answer to these questions, and to many more that could be
framed, is probably yes and no and as varied as the Pax men
and the times when they served. The men who sailed in 1951
undoubtedly had different motives and were in a different
stage in their lives than many who left for more specialized
places a decade or two later, and clearly the times had changed
dramatically from 1951 to 1976.[23]

It seems the best way to answer these questions is to observe what these men said about their experience after they

left Pax and also what they did. Kehler's research indicates that some returned to their former communities and occupations. Others pursued higher education and became professionals, some entering teaching and medicine. A number became pastors. But if the events and experiences at reunions of Pax units is any indication, they were all changed into more reflective, engaged, and responsive individuals, concerned about the plight of the world's people, more aware that all people are the children of God.

We conclude this chapter with the comments of selected Paxers from among the hundreds whose stories are just as dramatic. One research project conducted by a returned Paxer provides some examples. In 1989, Doug Klassen asked a number of Paxers, "What effect did your Pax experience have on you as a Person?"[24] One replied, "Those two years are etched in my memory. It gave me a 'world view' and many wonderful experiences and friendships. I now own those two years and they can't be taken away."

Another answered, "I grew very much spiritually, I realized it was good to work with people from other Mennonite Churches for one common cause and goal. I matured, realizing the world's needs and the love of Christians worldwide."

And another said, "It set a new course and direction for my life. It took me out of a small community to a more global view of life. Once I saw what our people were doing in the world, I became proud to be a Mennonite."

After three to five decades of reflection on their experience, in the year 2000 a number of Pax men were asked to evaluate their Pax experience by responding to three questions:[25] 1) Why did you go into Pax? 2) What were some of the most significant experiences you had in Pax? and 3) What do you think was the lasting importance of Pax? The nature and variety of assignments and relationships established are truly amazing.

Fremont Regier returned after his Pax experience to serve for a number of years in Africa in community development. Reflecting on his Pax experience after forty years, he said that

Midway through high school I received a very strong call to Christian service in Africa. Early in college I heard missionaries Archie and Erma Graber, from Congo speak and I asked them about future agricultural/medial service there. Archie encouraged me to come out to Congo then as a Pax man.

[One of the most meaningful impacts was] introduction to one small, but terribly significant part of Africa, an initial first exposure to a culture different from my own and an introduction to the intrigue of living cross-culturally, which instilled in me a very strong love and hunger for Africa, a profound appreciation for the universality of the gospel—a new concept to me as I observed Congolese Christians expressing their faith.

Pax provided an opportunity for young men to serve in a cross-cultural setting, an opportunity for young men to give an active, positive peace witness in lieu of military service, both during the service and afterwards, a sense of helping the Mennonite Church carry the peace witness and an opportunity to participate in, be a part of, the international Christian church.[26]

Arlin Hunsberger, whose Pax experience launched him into a life of international development remembers that

I first heard about Pax by reading the church papers. I was also aware that a man from our conference (Franconia) had returned from Pax Service. The idea of working in Europe intrigued me but I didn't think that I could go because of the cost. I was working as a butcher/meat cutter for a young businessman, Frank Keller, an avid supporter of MCC and its work. After discussing Pax with him and with his encouragement I began to think that it was worth exploring. At that time (1955) Pax fellows were expected to raise, if possible, the money to support themselves which was $75.00 per month. Frank felt so strongly about Pax that he offered to pay the costs for my first year and encouraged me to try to find support for the other year. My home congregation, Line Lexington Mennonite, immediately agreed to pay the $75.00 per month for the second year.

I went into Pax in Germany and worked in Backnang, building houses for about 6 months. One day Dwight Wiebe, European Pax Director, asked if I would go to Greece. I didn't have much of an idea as to what I was to do in Greece. Something was mentioned about food preservation/canning needs in Greece. Within a few days Don

Schierling (also from the Backnang unit) and I were on the train headed to Greece.

I believe that one of the most meaningful aspects of our work had to do with relating to the refugees who came to live in the constructed houses at Backnang. During evening visits with them they would relate their first-hand experiences in coming to the West—and after getting better acquainted would describe some of their terrifying wartime experiences. To a young, naive Pennsylvanian this made a profound impression on me.

I remember one evening going to visit an elderly widow, who lived with her son who seldom spoke because of having been severely traumatized during the war. When she opened the door a crack and saw me she quickly said that she didn't want to buy anything. She thought I was a salesperson. When she found that I simply came to visit with her and her son she seemed shocked and immediately brought coffee, cake and cookies and talked non-stop. I had been her first visitor during the year or more that she lived there.

Very quickly after entering the Pax unit it became evident that there were many different groups of Mennonites and they all could (at least in Pax) work together very well. I learned much about the different groups and was able to trust and feel comfortable with the Pax fellows many of whom came from different stripes of Mennonites from those with whom I had been acquainted.

Working in Tsakones, Greece was totally different from working in Germany. Working in a significantly different culture meant that we had to relate to people from a position of trying to learn the basics of the culture and to not force our preconceived ideas regarding that culture on them. The predominant Greek Orthodox religion also gave me the opportunity to observe a different, from what I was used to, form of religion. I also learned to worship in a different way and, gradually, very meaningful way.

After completing two years in Greece, I was asked to be co-director of a Mennonite Voluntary Service Work Camp in Berlin. These work camps placed young people from different cultures and countries together to work and live together. Many of the participants came from countries that were not friendly toward each other nor did they respect each other.

This animosity of course, was transmitted to the young people in the group and it was necessary to work through conflicts, which very often surfaced. We were all forced to work together and to compromise. Working in this area of leadership certainly broadened my thinking and awareness regarding conflict stemming from cultural and historical differences.

I believe that the Pax program played a crucial role in exposing many young people of the church to the broader needs of people throughout the world. It was a powerful instrument in getting people out of their close, sometimes almost closed, communities into situations that made them ponder and search for different ways of moving through life.

I seriously doubt that if I had not gone into Pax, that I would have ever gone to college and had the opportunity of serving further with MCC in Haiti, being on the faculty of Goshen College, or having the opportunity of working in International Development programs such as the Pan American Development Foundation's environmental program in Haiti.

Robert Mullet, a Pax man who learned three different languages and served in several different parts of the world including Haiti and Afghanistan, credits his Pax experience as a major factor in his life.

I first became aware of Pax when one of the older youth in our church in Red Top did a term of Pax service (I believe it was in Africa). I somehow knew from the time I was a little kid that I would do a term of service overseas with MCC after finishing college. Growing up in Dawson County, Montana, I hadn't had much of a chance to see the world. Pax seemed like a good way to do that.

In high school and college I found I had a real liking for and ability to learn foreign languages, so a term of service overseas also seemed like a good opportunity to use that talent. I ended up in Haiti simply because that's what position MCC offered me. Even though I knew Spanish well, I was glad for the chance to go to Haiti, since it meant an opportunity to improve my French.

Our decision to go to Afghanistan was a conscious one—my wife and I wanted to go somewhere neither my wife nor I had been, so we'd have an even start.

Pax provided many meaningful experiences, although it's been long enough that it's difficult to sort out which I'd put at the top of the list. Here's a short sampling: In Haiti, it was the practice of the MCC unit in Grande Riviere to put on a Christmas program for the hospital staff. Both Christmases I was there I translated a Christmas play into Creole, and we performed it. It was lots of fun working with Haitian friends to get the translation correct—as well as performing it.

Some friends and I did a 90-mile, cross-country hike, through some really remote parts of Haiti. We ended up walking all night the second night before we finally arrived at our destination.

Most of my memories from Afghanistan revolve around activities we enjoyed with the rest of the foreign community. Since contact with Afghans was limited (proselytizing could get you either expelled from the country or killed) most of our leisure time was spent with the rather large international community. We got to be in sports (tennis tournaments, flag football, softball, and basketball) and also performed in several musicals. It was a lot of fun—and part of the dynamic was the chance to associate with many different nationalities in the process.

We did become good friends with one of our language teachers, named Malek. His wife became pregnant, and he called us when she went into labor since we had a vehicle and he didn't. When we arrived at the gates of the maternity hospital Malek, as an Afghan male, was not allowed to enter. Myself, as a foreigner, was somehow exempt from that rule, so I could go on in. The same thing happened when she was released from the hospital—so we got to see the mother and baby before the husband did. Strange.

In my opinion, the significant effect of the Pax experience was more felt by the Pax personnel who went, and the "leavening" influence of their home communities when they returned. I think positive things happened in their places of service, but I'm skeptical of how much permanent change resulted. In my case specifically, the hospital I worked in Haiti was finally turned back to the government by MCC after about 15 years. It's barely functioning now, since the government doesn't have the resources to keep it going. The hospital in Kabul where we worked was destroyed in the civil war that occurred there after we left. It is my impression that things are much worse there now than when we worked there in the 70's.

Halfway across the globe from Afghanistan, Harley Showalter served as a Pax man in Bolivia along with several fellow Pax men on loan to the Methodist church:

My uncle, Luke Rhodes, was in the first Pax unit to serve in Germany in the refugee housing construction. This I became aware of Pax quite early. Then my cousin Glen Showalter became a Pax man in Greece in the late 1950s. So I volunteered. I wanted badly to go to Europe and enjoy some of the historic spots, and work with needs of a people whose heritage was more like my own. But MCC told me that Europe was a priority 3, Latin America (Bolivia) a priority 1, and as I recall, Africa was a priority 2. I argued with MCC-Akron about the needs of Bolivia, a country I knew little about. I accepted the location with reluctance, but was later grateful for this decision

My assignment was to be "on loan to the Methodist Mission in Bolivia," a campus outpost in a frontier town of Montero, some 80 kilometers north of the large city of Santa Cruz. The Colegio Metodista de Montero featured a secondary school, a seminary, and was the point from where other Paxmen on loan to the Methodists launched outpost calls of duty in Quatro Ojitos, Yapacani, Portachuelo, and other points.

My assignment in Montero was to help with several projects: giving care to Heifer Project animals transported from North America; introducing pastures/legumes for animal forage; developing rations for their care and health; keeping a watchful eye for ticks, screw worm, hoof and mouth disease. These were typical tropical adjustment problems as North American animals were very stressed and needed to be quarantined until some adjustments could be made (until they could enjoy new rations and some assessments could be done on desirability of particular breeds of cattle, hogs, donkeys, and fowl for the climate and conditions).

The most meaningful aspects of Pax included the great opportunity to learn a new culture. This leads one to recognize that human experience is guided by a "world view" and that mine is one of many. I learned much about the Methodist tradition, and to know some wonderful

Methodist people. My work in Bolivia also brought me into relationship with the Mennonite Colonists living in the frontiers, and acquainted me with Mennonites in Canada, Paraguay, Brazil, and Mexico.

Connecting with other volunteers from other parts of the United States and Canada was a great experience. I developed meaningful relationships, which I would never have had otherwise. I received much more than I gave. The Pax program gave me an opportunity to relate to others in the larger world. It should still be a vital program today, but the conditions involving the draft and conscription are gone. Unfortunately Pax died!

To this very day, I am grateful for having volunteered two years of my life in Bolivia. I returned to the United States a more mature and determined person: formal education became more meaningful, the benefit of a second language (Spanish) assists me to this day, and I appreciate cultural diversity in America as each lends beauty and a life of its own to us North Americans. I have encouraged other youth to take advantage of cross-cultural experiences. Unfortunately, the Pax program died!

Calvin J. King worked in a part of the world that is now as deeply immersed in developing nationhood as it was thirty years ago—Timor.

I first became aware of the Pax program as a young person still in High School when Dalton Hostetler entered the program. Dalton and I were from the same church (Pleasant Valley Mennonite, Harper, KS). The draft board of Harper County was not sympathetic to COs and always referred applicants for CO status to the state draft board, who then would do a thorough investigation. However, when they learned of the type of service Dalton was planning to do, the local draft board granted his request without further hassle.

The second influence were friends I made in college, both Hesston and Goshen, who had served in the program. I admired their experience, their dedication to service and commitment to Christ and the church.

The most meaningful aspects of my Pax experience included identifying and walking with local Christians. My assignment in Timor was with an agricultural training school, owned/operated by the local Protestant church, but developed with MCC/CWS resources. Earlier workers had developed the land and location for the school.

By the time I arrived, Pax men spent the majority of their time in the gardens of students, or working together in the several hectares operated by the school. Whites in Timor and in Indonesia were often identified as "orang Belanda" or Dutch, a carryover from the colonial past. I often heard expressions of surprise that I would get my hands dirty, or that I would physically work hard to accomplish a task. To work side by side in the gardening projects demonstrated that something different was going on here.

Seeing that our project was making an identifiable difference in the food resources of the region was also very meaningful. MCC had been invited by the local Protestant church to help develop the food supply of local Christians. Being one of the eastern islands where corn is the staple, and the growing season often four months or less, they were prone to periods of famine. The idea of the agricultural training school was to bring young men from the mountains of Timor and nearby islands to spend a year learning basic gardening skills. Students were given their own plot to cultivate, and to keep the proceeds. The idea was that the students would then return to their homes and practice what they had learned, along with some of the improved seeds which we brought from North America.

In addition to the student gardens, we had about two hectares, which we used to generate income for the school. Students were expected to work here as well. During my years, an improved variety of corn was introduced which increased corn production considerably. I understand in the years that have passed since, the corn production throughout the region is considerably improved.

One of the things I learned while I was still there was that students were not eager to return home. When asked why, they would say, why should I go home, work hard and raise a nice garden, then be obligated to "feed the whole family." They found the village life near Kupang, and money in their pockets, a good life style.

Without intending to teach them to be capitalists or entrepreneurs, yet in fact this is what happened. We saw that our project made a difference, often with unintended consequences, in the lives of those we worked with.

When I visited Timor three years ago, I was privileged to visit with a number of former students. Those reunions were filled with words of appreciation for the place the school had in their lives. Several had done quite well, including one who is now the village head, overseeing agricultural matters of his region.

From the vantage point of almost three decades hence, I believe the Pax program made it possible for young men to put their faith into action, a creative alternative to military service. It focused on the real needs of human kind, whatever the location, and Pax men walked patiently seeking to bring their common dreams into reality.

Even though it is clear that the "works of compassion" the Pax men performed speak more eloquently than any words, these reminiscences of Pax men, expressed some forty years after their time of service, are also very persuasive. They are words that come from having remembered, relived, and reflected about what they had seen, felt, and done many years earlier. Almost to a person, Pax men maintain that they received much more than they gave. It is almost impossible not to remind ourselves that the Pax men experienced first-hand the axiom Jesus laid down two millennia ago: "He that loses his life for my sake will find it" (Luke 9:24).

The Impact of Pax on MCC

It has been suggested that even though Pax was terminated, it must have had a significant impact on MCC. There is little direct information on this question.

However, there is an assumption that Teachers Abroad Program (TAP) was a fairly direct consequence of the Pax experience. The evidence of Pax experience being transferred to TAP is not convincing. The records of the beginnings of TAP state, "When the MCC, together with the Mennonite Mission Secretaries and the Council of Mennonite and Affiliated Colleges decided, in 1961, that they could not participate in the Peace Corps program, they began to seek ways in which their own program could accommodate new service possibilities."[27] Pax is not mentioned in any of the discussions.

The Peace Corps had presented a very attractive alternative to Mennonite young people, for numerous youth served

`

in it. Consequently, a consultation held in September 1961 spelled out the reasons why Mennonites could not whole-heartedly cooperate. Reservations included the restrictions against proselytizing, the recruitment practices that took the selective process away from the church, and the policy of operation which made the Peace Corps an arm of the government.[28]

The main focus of TAP was providing an avenue of opportunity for a strong tradition of service among Mennonites, namely the teaching profession. While the Pax program included community education as a major aspect of its development work phase, this was not teaching in the professional sense. TAP emerged as an outlet for the professionally-trained graduates from the Mennonite colleges. Indirectly, the Pax model undoubtedly influenced the emergence of TAP in the shape of single volunteers going abroad, serving in a variety of situations, with great creativity, often alone. As with Pax, however, this almost always was a result of MCC activities in the locality. It may well be that other MCC programs have been influenced by the Pax model, but further research will be needed to bring the connection to light.

Chapter 8

Pax on the World Stage

In the Introduction, Al Keim suggests that there is a direct connection between the emergence of the Pax vision and the profound, world-shaking events bracketed by the beginning of the Korean and the conclusion of the Vietnam wars. And of course the World War II experiences with alternative service, which were less than ideal, prepared the way for the idea of Pax.

Dedication of first group of Mennonite Refugee homes in Espelkamp, 1952. Otto Wiebe, German Refugee settlement officer, giving message. Calvin W. Redekop photo

Further, as Keim suggests, post World War II political, cultural, and social conditions and developments provided the impetus for MCC's constituency to become involved in the larger social issues of our times. Thus, the MCC workers in Europe and the personnel at the home office on the mainland played their respective roles in Pax, being the right persons at the right "time and season." Together they connected the various strands together to make the fabric out of which Pax was to be born. The specific persons involved in the conception, implementation, and administration of Pax could easily have been any other set of persons.[1]

112

Reflections on the Pax Role in Larger Society

In hindsight it is possible to postulate that pacifist Mennonite society, best known for its withdrawal from the secular affairs of the world, had been dramatically influenced by the turmoil in the world. Quite possibly the innovative Pax was a predictable result. This is difficult to prove, but I believe it to be true. The well known dissatisfaction with the Civilian Public Service (CPS) program on the part of many of the CPS men—"working on jobs that appeared insignificant had a demoralizing effect on many men"[2]—bears this out.

The range of CPS work included helping on farms, dairy testing, soil conservation work, forest service, mental hospitals, and guinea pig experiments. So the mood was established to demand an improvement in the relevance of alternative service to military service.

Pax can also be seen as a necessary outcome of the history and theology of the Mennonite society. This tradition is expressed in individual disciples' desire to be relevant and to make a sacrifice if necessary, a stance nurtured by the community of faith. It explains the presence of the Canadian Pax men who did not face the draft but had experienced a similar community. A story such as Pax must consider the faith struggle of individuals, nurtured in their respective faith communities, as they react to a particular environment. This conclusion applies equally to the non-Mennonite/BIC Pax men who served, including members of Church of the Brethren men and several Quakers.

Pax certainly reflected the changes in the psyche of the Mennonite and related communities. Alongside the other expressions of compassion and concern that were rapidly emerging, Pax expressed the awakening desire to be a worthy member of the human community. Consequently, the Pax program was a kind of "spontaneous combustion" of the Mennonite community which had decided that exemption from military service by the most painless means would no longer satisfy. Mennonites began to balance the need to remain separate and nonconformed to the world with the need to be relevant and responsible to society in exchange for the privilege of being a peculiar and separated people.

In short, the two kingdoms theology and position was being re-evaluated. Perry Bush has proposed that

> Mennonites responded to the social dislocation of war out of a genuine sense of Christian concern and commitment. Yet is it also true that through such benevolent efforts Mennonites expressed their aspirations to citizenship, when because of the calling of the Mennonite heritage, the accepted routes of fighting and dying for their country were closed to them. They would overcome the negativity of their military refusal by their sacrificial giving and service; their good works would prove their worthiness as Americans.

Bush adds that

> P. C. Hiebert executive secretary [sic] chairman of the MCC, [stated, circa 1945], "Mennonites seized the chance to disprove the charges of cowardice and selfishness made against the conscientious objectors and to express in a positive, concrete way the principles of peace and goodwill." No longer did being Mennonite mean an inwardly focused orientation on the theological and cultural patterns of isolated Mennonite world. Mennonitism involved an active, caring aspect as well—an image of compassionate concern for the needy.[3]

Pax and the Peace Corps

Rumors have persisted in Mennonite circles that the Peace Corps, originally headed up by President Kennedy's brother-in-law Sargent Shriver, was inspired in part by the example of the Pax program.

The evidence is sparse. The most specific claim for this connection is J. Winfield Fretz's article, "Peace Corps: Child of the Historic Peace Churches." After taking a broader approach on how the historic peace churches proposed alternatives to war during World War II, including the voluntary service movement, Fretz states that "it was in the light of this general background that much of the character of the Peace Corps was developed."[4]

After describing the Peace Corps, Fretz opens a section entitled "The Peace Corps and Pax" and states that "There are interesting similarities and contrasts between the proposed

Peace Corps and the Pax program of the Mennonite Central Committee."[5] But Fretz is careful not to say that the Peace Corps was not directly inspired by Pax.

Reflecting the same orientation, James Juhnke, who recently returned from Pax service in Germany, stated in a Bethel College talk that

> Pax is valuable as an example. One aspect of Pax as an example comes from an unexpected source. The United States government has adopted a Point Four Youth Corps program of young Americans to work on assistance projects in foreign countries. Pax Services can serve a precedent for the work ability and value of such a program.[6]

He also does not imply a direct causal relationship.

The various accounts of the sources of the ideas for the Peace Corps are inconclusive and vague and no direct links between the Peace Corps and the MCC Pax program have come to light.[7] On the contrary, Peace Corps documentation alludes to many sources, including William James' idea of "A Moral Equivalent of War," by which he proposed an "army conscripted for war against poverty, ignorance, and disease";[8] and Franklin Delano Roosevelt's "three-pronged youth resources effort: the Civilian Conservation Corps (CCC), the Works Projects Administration (WPA), and the National Youth Administration (NYA)," which gave hope and inspired an entire generation of young people.[9] American churches, both Catholic and Protestant, had also been active in relief and service activities during the great depression and sent young people abroad in a variety of humanitarian services.

The basic idea of the Peace Corps originated with Congressman Henry S. Reuss and Senator Hubert Humphrey. As early as January 1960, Reuss had proposed a bill in the House of Representatives to study establishing a Point Four Youth Corps. Later that month Senator Richard L. Neuberger proposed a similar bill in the Senate. In June 1960, when Humphrey proposed a bill for the creation of an agency in which young Americans could serve in missions overseas, he actually used the name "Peace Corps" in proposing the bill.[10]

The most direct relationship between Pax and the Peace Corps is probably provided by the International Voluntary

Service organization (IVS). It is quite clear that IVS, under the charismatic leadership of Don Luce, was the most direct inspiration for the Peace Corps.[11] Roy Hoopes concurs, saying,

> The organization most often described as the real prototype of the Peace Corps is the International Voluntary Services. IVS was formed in 1953, to some extent as an effort to reorganize and give more specific direction to all American missionary programs. It is governed by a board composed of both Catholic and Protestant representatives.[12]

In a speech to Congress on June 15, 1960, entitled, "Establishment of Peace Corps," Hubert Humphrey referred to the International Voluntary Service experience as a model for the Peace Corps, stating,

> Mr. President, I wish briefly to allude to the International Voluntary Service, the organization which has the experience most directly relevant to the proposed Peace Corps. IVS is a private nonprofit organization, and it takes contracts from ICA and foundations. These idealistic, talented young men are oriented toward the people-to-people approach, and according to every account, they have enjoyed extraordinary success.[13]

In 1963, William Snyder, secretary of IVS for twenty years, reported in a memorandum to the MCC Executive Committee, "At the last IVS meeting, Russell Stevenson was asked about the role of IVS in bringing the Peace Corps into existence." Snyder then referred to the Humphrey speech noted above as evidence for the role of IVS.

There can be little doubt that Pax was known in IVS circles, to other religious voluntary service program boards and committees, and that it was probably brought to Humphrey's and other government officials' attention. But given the Pax program's relative newness (only nine years old),[14] minuscule size, and history, Pax could not have possessed much of a reputation or image.

If church service programs and, most specifically, the Mennonite Voluntary service program and Pax, were cited or alluded to in the Peace Corp discussion, it was certainly Hubert H. Humphrey who brought them to the attention of those dreaming about the Peace Corps.

Wingebach supports this observation: "Humphrey was an early backer of the Corps. Impressed by the success of the Quaker (American Friends Service Committee), he had tested its appeal before college groups on several occasions in 1957."[15] As is well known by contemporaries, the Mennonite Central Committee voluntary service program and the Pax program were much larger than the Friends program, but the AFSC had been much more successful in promoting and publicizing its programs than the Mennonites.[16]

Pax may also have influenced the Peace Corps through General Lewis B. Hershey. According to Hoopes,

> In 1953, the founders of IVS (which included William T. Snyder, executive secretary of MCC) went to General Lewis B. Hershey, Director of Selective Service, to see what could be done about obtaining draft deferment for IVS volunteers.[17]

Hershey had visited the Pax and MVS programs in l951 to report to Congress on the legitimacy of extending alternative service credit—not deferment—to COs serving overseas. So it is certainly possible that Hershey mentioned the Pax idea in his discussions with IVS officials and the persons President Kennedy commissioned to initiate the Peace Corps.

It is clear that Pax can claim some inspiration and experience, which contributed to the creation of the IVS. The description of the IVS volunteers sounds suspiciously like the requirements for Pax. As Hoopes states,

> IVS started work primarily in rural areas at first. In fact, IVS would take only boys who had been raised on a farm or who had agricultural-college training. IVS volunteers are offered a two-year contract. During this time they are guaranteed all necessary expenses, including transportation to and from the assigned projects, housing, subsistence, clothing allowance, medical care, insurance, and an annual thirty-day vacation. IVS volunteers always work under the general guidance of American technicians overseas; their primary objective is to establish good will and understanding through being good neighbors.[18]

It is probably justifiable to conclude that Pax affected IVS thinking and conceptualization, which in turn informed the Peace Corps proposals.

Further historical information linking Pax with the Peace
Corps is MCC's testimony during the hearings leading up to
the establishment of the Peace Corps. The hearings on June 22
and 23, 1961, included the following account:

> Statement of C. N. Hostetter, Jr., Chairman, Mennonite
> Central Committee, Akron, Pa.
> I am C. N. Hostetter, Chairman of the Mennonite Cen-
> tral Committee, one of America's church-related relief agen-
> cies, organized in 1920. As one phase of our foreign relief and
> service program 10 years ago, we began a pax (sic) or peace
> team program—*pax* is Latin term for peace. In these 10 years,
> 460 young men have served two- to three-year terms in 26
> foreign countries. Their work has been similar to that envi-
> sioned in the Peace Corps program. We commend and ap-
> prove the emphasis that seeks to promote better understand-
> ing of other peoples on the part of America and a better un-
> derstanding of America by other peoples of the world.[19]

Hostetter continued, providing some illustrations of the
work Pax men were doing. "In Paraguay seven young men
work on the Paraguay Government and United States Government trans-Chaco roadway project. In Nepal seven young
men skilled in construction are working with Nepalese, building hospitals and schools."[20] It seems likely that William T.
Snyder, Lewis B. Hershey, and C. N. Hostetter probably provided the most direct personal testimonies and support of the
Pax vision as it might relate to the proposed Peace Corps.

As the Peace Corps planners moved into action, men who
had served in IVS and Pax received questionnaires. Although
the form is not dated, it was apparently sent out in 1960 and
administered by the American Institute for Research in Washington, D.C. Numerous Pax men reported receiving the form.
The intent of the survey is stated in the introduction:

> The purpose of this study is to gather factual accounts of
> events, which have occurred in the course of American ex-
> perience during overseas assignments. We are collecting
> this information for use in selection and training for the
> Peace Corps.[21]

The questionnaire continued, "We are interested in incidents
in which the American or someone he actually observed did

something that was particularly effective or ineffective in getting something done."

The Mennonite Central Committee spent considerable time and effort evaluating the new Peace Corps program. This came into focus at a meeting held May 11-13, 1961, in Chicago and included Mennonite Mission Board Secretaries, the Council of Mennonite and Affiliated Colleges, and the Mennonite Central Committee Executive Committee. At this time, "the Mennonite Central Committee was requested to explore possible avenues of cooperation."[22] Before the conference, William T. Snyder and Robert Miller, of MCC along with J. Winfield Fretz, had visited and consulted with Gordon Boyce, Director of Private Agency Relations for the Peace Corps, and other Peace Corps officials in Washington, D. C.

They reported that "One of the main programs of the Peace Corps will be contracts with private agencies."[23] Their report also included some concerns: "We have accepted support from the governments in the nature of surplus commodities and ocean freight reimbursement, but can we conscientiously accept support for personnel?" and "Can we meet the requirement of 'open' recruitment and assignment within our personnel policies and program administration?"[24]

The cautions notwithstanding, within months three proposals for Peace Corps funding in Greece, Jerusalem, and Bolivia were drawn up.[25] The Greece proposal had an annual budget of $52,000 and centered on expansion of the program by ten men. The Jerusalem application contained a budget of $26,700 and featured two additional men and several vehicles, while the Bolivia project suggested a $43,800 budget and aimed at sending two teams of four men each into the Santa Cruz region to do rural agricultural and settlement work.[26]

But the applications were either not formally submitted, or were withdrawn, for on September 16, 1961, the following Executive Committee action was adopted:

> It appears inadvisable for MCC and its constituent agencies to enter into contract with the Peace Corps program. Three reasons are preventing church agencies from participation: (1) the stated policy against proselytizing [sic] with its implied restriction on Christian witnessing; (2) the re-

sulting policy which denies the church agency a satisfactory measure of selectivity in choosing candidates, and (3) the policy of operation which constitutes the agency as an arm of the government. It seems evident that the worthy goals envisioned by this program can be achieved to a higher degree through support and expansion of the programs of missions, relief, Pax, Voluntary Service, etc. as now sponsored by the churches and MCC.[27]

That the Pax approach could "achieve the worthy goals envisioned by the Peace Corps run by the federal government to a higher degree" as stated by the MCC Executive Committee cited above, is further illustrated by Larry Kehler, writing,

> The Peace Corps program was met with enthusiasm in church circles when it was first introduced. However this has given way to a much more "subdued attitude toward the venture." R. Sargent Shriver Jr. director of the Peace Corps, estimates that it will cost about $9,000-10,000 a year to maintain one Peace Corps worker abroad. (Compare this to the $900 which it takes to support an MCC Paxman abroad for one year).[28]

The Contributions of Pax to the Mennonite World

But even if Pax did not have a direct influence on the idea of the Peace Corps as it did on IVS, that does not diminish its wider importance. One glimmer of possible wider if subtle impact is the February 1959 *Euro Pax News* report that Dr. Bues of the German Labor Ministry visited the Enkenbach Pax Unit. "He was apparently looking for models for a prospective German alternative system program. It seems likely that the Pax program helped lead the German government into an alternative service program that included the possibility of overseas service for conscientious objectors to war."[29]

More research must be done to discover whether Pax had any influence on the German alternative service program. However, it would certainly be a fitting capstone to the commitment of Pax men who gave of themselves so enthusiastically. On a more modest scale, it is fairly clear that the Pax program played a role in the German Mennonite Peace movement as the following report indicates:

Leaders of the German Mennonite congregations took quick action when the German "Bundestag" adopted a law reintroducing conscription on July 8, 1956. Two weeks later they founded the German Mennonite Peace Committee in Ludwigshafen. They defined two tasks for the new committee: reintroducing and strengthening the Christian peace witness in and through congregations and counseling and supporting conscientious objectors. Since then the German Mennonite Peace Committee has sought to do justice to the mandate—at times in cooperation at times in tension—with the congregations.[30]

That this reflects the example of Pax, which the German Mennonites had seen in action for four years, is clear. This is reflected further in the report: After many discussions, in a "decision also reached in 1985, the 'Vereinigung' recommends conscientious objection to young conscripts and encourages the congregations to engage in active peace education and peace service." The Pax men, as well as the many MCC workers who had been in Germany since 1947 helped to prepare the ground for the re-adoption of the historic peace position.

Thus whether or not we grant that there are numerous similarities in goals and philosophy as well as possible influences between the programs of IVS, Peace Corps, and possibly even German national and Mennonite conscientious objector programs and Pax, we can say that Pax was a unique compassionate response to human need and suffering in a specific time in history beginning with helping fellow members of the Anabaptist tradition but quickly expanding to include victims of many parts of the world.

In the Future: International Mennonite Pax Corps?

Just a bit more than a month before he died, during a November 1999 planning committee meeting for the fiftieth birthday of the Pax idea, Dwight Wiebe, the third director of the European Pax program, asked, "Why did Pax not survive to become a permanent international force, such as the Peace Corps?" He wondered whether the witness for peace and reconciliation was waning in the Anabaptist-Mennonite household of faith.

There may be many reasons for the apparent demise of the international Pax movement, but it can be suggested that a small religious movement, now totaling a few more than a million members worldwide, inheriting a history of martyrdom and marginalization and thus still attempting to establish an identity in a dramatically modernizing and changing world, could not be mount such a major effort on an ongoing basis. The denomination may simply be too small for such a venture.

On the one hand, it has been suggested that the specific niche that the Pax movement filled is no longer extant. The post-World War period included massive refugee displacements and resultant need for new housing; the emergence of independent nation states all over the world, but especially in Africa and the East whose appeals for help were everywhere; and the conflict between communism and the so-called "Free World." Such factors provided the context in which Pax was able to provide timely help. But this era seemed to have drawn to a close about the time the Vietnam War ended.

But on the other hand, the vision of an international voluntary service organization is not an impossible one. It is at least possible to conceive of an organization which would enlist young men and women from Anabaptist-oriented fellowships all over the world to keep the witness of Christ's peace through service to all, regardless of race, creed, nationality, or the particular world conditions.

There is interest in developing a Mennonite world communion and a global Mennonite Central Committee. Meanwhile an international Mennonite voluntary service (IMVS) already operated in a limited fashion in the early 1950s in Europe, including the Greece project; South America, especially in Paraguay and Bolivia; and elsewhere. Amid such factors, who would insist some form of IMVS is not a possibility?[31]

In any case, it is reassuring that there continues to unfold much humanitarian and peace-oriented contribution through such ongoing organizations as the Peace Corps, International Voluntary Service, American Friends Service Committee, Brethren Service Commission, Church World Service, and literally hundreds of private and religious organizations. All of these are performing some of the tasks that Pax provided.

The termination of Pax should not imply any diminishment of its contribution. It made its mark in history—the fact that Pax ended merely reminds us that history provides almost infinite examples of the mysterious working together of a variety of conditions and events and responses, some of which become institutionalized, others not.

Pax is one of those "creative eruptions," a short one-act play whose actors appeared on the stage at a critical turning point in human history and, with considerable drama at some points in the plot, acted out a practical and symbolic message of peace and reconciliation in "the name of Christ," a drama which had occasionally been expressed earlier in other forms by a minority group—the Anabaptists. It has often been said that this minority group has had an impact out of proportion to its numerical strength. But the danger of hubris causes us to wear this accolade lightly. Thus the players in this one act, *The Pax Story*, want simply to be remembered with the many others who have served in other equally noble tasks in history.

The Pax idea and its fulfillment could only happen because of the long historical saga of a people that tenaciously maintained a faithfulness to a vision which saw a city to be built on a hill, a kingdom which was going to be built by Christ's followers, but only if they remained true to his teachings, which proclaimed the love of God and neighbor as the twin pillars of salvation.

But is it reasonable to believe that the kind of vision and dedication, and collective effort will be repeated again? Social commentators remind us that the rampant individualism reflected at present in the post modernism age of relativism and deconstructionism will not allow this kind of energy to emerge. But history continues to exhibit marvelous eruptions of hope when times were darkest.

The yearning and struggle for peace and reconciliation, a goal all humanity has shared through the ages, continues.

> Ring out the narrowing lust of Gold
> Ring out the thousand wars of old
> Ring in the thousand years of peace
>
> —*Tennyson*, "In Memoriam"

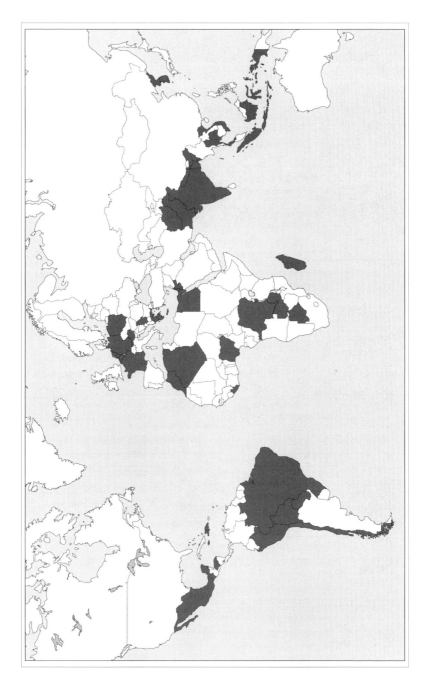

Shaded areas show the worldwide scope of the Pax effort.

BASIC CLOTHING LIST FOR MEN IN I-W BUILDERS UNIT (West Germany)[1]

LUGGAGE
1 foot locker
1 large suitcase

CLOTHING
1 overcoat
1 raincoat
1 dress suit
1 pair wool pants (dress)
4 pair work trousers or 4 sets combination shirt and washable pants
1 jacket (work)
1 jacket (dress)
1 white dress shirt
3 colored dress shirts
2 work shirts
2 T shirts
2 long wool underwear
6 pair summer weight underwear
3 pair wool socks
5 pair light weight socks (durable)
1 pair dress oxfords
1 pair work shoes (G. I. type)
1 pair rubbers
2 pair flannel pajamas
2 pair light colored pajamas
10 handkerchiefs—white and colored

1 pair warm dress gloves
2 pair work gloves (leather)
GENERAL
1 blanket, 3 sheets, 1 pair pillow slips
6 towels, 6 washcloths
3 bars soap
shaving supplies
flashlight
pocket knife
hat and cap
first aid kit (small)
shoe shine kit
sewing kit
stationery supplies

DESIRABLE (not furnished by MCC)
watch, fountain pen, camera and film, diary

NOTE It is desirable to keep luggage as light as possible. You may find it convenient to take a duffel bag (with locks) instead of a foot locker. This list need not be followed in detail, but it is given merely as a general suggestive list. Clothing does not need to be new but it should be durable and in good condition. When making purchases, your own personal tastes will have to be considered.

Appendix B

Alternative Service[2]

Alternative service was the term used to describe the program of civilian service available for conscientious objectors from 1952 until shortly after the end of the draft in December 1972. (The final draft inductions and work orders came in the last six months of 1972.) In lieu of induction into the armed forces they were required to perform "civilian work contributing to the maintenance of the national health, safety, or interest."

The Selective Training and Service Act of 1940, in effect during World War II, expired in March 1947. In June 1948, a new Selective Service law was enacted. This legislation, the first peacetime conscription in U.S. history, at first provided for the deferment of conscientious objectors. The act was extended by the U.S. Congress in 1950, but increasing draft calls resulting from U.S. participation in the Korean War and vocal opposition to deferment brought an end in 1952 to the short period of freedom for objectors.

Even while advocating continued deferments for conscientious objectors in 1951, church leaders connected with the National Service Board for Religious Objectors (National Interreligious Service Board for Conscientious Objectors) offered specific suggestions for an alternative service program during meetings with legislators and Selective Service officials. An amendment that removed the provision for deferment of conscientious objectors was added to the draft laws in May 1951, but final plans for an alternative service program were not put in effect until President Truman signed in February 1952, an executive order that described the work obligations of conscientious objectors.

Neither the Selective Service administrators nor the church agencies favored the use of national work camps on the Civilian Public Service pattern of World War II. Under the new provisions, conscientious objectors were required to perform civilian duties either for the U.S. government, for nonprofit charitable and service organizations, or for public health, welfare, and educational projects. The period of service was twenty-four months. Brethren and Mennonite leaders offered to help find suitable jobs for alternative service assignees. The American Friends Service Committee decided not to participate in alternative service plans because the committee was unwilling "to be a party to the success of the conscription operation."

During the period that alternative service requirements were in effect, most men classified as conscientious objectors available for service (I-W) chose alternative service in preference to military duty or a prison sentence for non-cooperation with the draft. The types of work projects to which they could be assigned included work with children or young people, community work, educational projects, conservation work, government service, work in health-related fields, legal assistance, local church projects, work in communications media and the arts, peace education, and various research projects.

A small percentage of the assignees served overseas, often in war-ravaged countries, where they aided refugees and worked in relief and rehabilitation projects.

Appendix C

Aims of the Pax Program³

These first four aims were stated in the Pax Handbook produced in 1952.
1. We aim to provide projects that offer opportunities to alleviate human need, tension, give encouragement to those less fortunate than we in undeveloped areas of the world, or help resettle and rehabilitate the displaced peoples in various parts of the world.

2. We aim to provide an opportunity for self growth for the worker himself by working with his hands serving and helping a people in need, and working with a people of another background and culture (altogether entered into in the right spirit is education indeed).

3. It is our aim and hope that the total impact will help to promote international goodwill and understanding as we work together with citizens of other countries in a spirit of sharing and brotherly love.

4. It is our aim and hope that the total impact will help to bring about in our church constituency a greater consciousness and a fuller realization of the suffering and the hopelessness found in a soul-sick world while in contrast we will see (sic) our own spiritual opportunities and our abundance of material wealth which we so often take for granted."

Purposes of the Pax Program
The following statement, clearly a revision of the earlier statement, is taken from a release simply entitled PAX, without a date.⁴
• to help with projects that offer opportunities to alleviate human needs and tensions in various parts of the world
• to provide an opportunity for a positive Christian witness by the individual, and the unit
• to provide opportunities for self-development
• to promote international goodwill and understanding by working with citizens of other countries in a spirit of brotherly love
• to bring to the church constituency a greater consciousness and fuller realization of the suffering and hopelessness found in the world, thus helping Americans be better stewards of their spiritual opportunities and abundance of material wealth.

Appendix D:
Diagram of MCC-Pax Organizational Structure

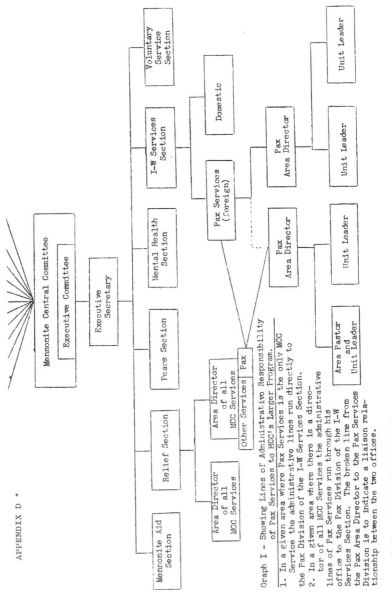

APPENDIX D *

Graph I – Showing Lines of Administrative Responsibility of Pax Services to MCC's Larger Program.

1. In a given area where Pax Services is the only MCC Service the administrative lines run directly to the Pax Division of the I-W Services Section.

2. In a given area where there is a director of all MCC Services the administrative lines of Pax Services run through his office to the Pax Division of the I-W Services Section. The broken line from the Pax Area Director to the Pax Services Division is to indicate a liaison relationship between the two offices.

* from PAX HANDBOOK 1952

Appendix E

Wilbur Maust Diary

1. Mid-June, 1956. Left on the Zuiderkreuz with about 15 to 18 Paxers for Germany. Late June I was assigned to a building unit in Bechterdiessen.

2. Dec. 8. Left Bechterdiessen for Kaiserslautern enroute to Vienna to work with Hungarian refugees. [On December 4 Wiebe announced that a wagonload of Paxers would be leaving (soon) for Vienna. Arlo Kasper, Jim Besse, Bob Good, Dean Hartman and Wilbur Maust were to be ready to leave. "Personnel, not supplies, needed for Vienna." We were to set up MCC "lagers" (camps) with several Paxers in each. Specific duties to be assign later.]

3. Dec. 11. At the camp in Ranzenbach bei Klausen Leopoldsdorf about 30 kms. from Vienna. Plans were to have 30 refugees with 4 Pax staff—refugees to stay 5-10 days then move on to the U.S. Plans were for 24,000 refugees to go to the U.S. before the New Year. Pax staff at Ranzenbach included Dean Hartman, leader, c/o bookkeeping, supplies, p.r., general running of the camp. Harold Hamm c/o recreation and keeping everyone occupied. David Hershberger (a new Pax arrival) c/o lighting the kerosene lamps, keep 10 wood stoves fired, help the matron in the kitchen when needed. W. Maust c/o immigration services: register refugees at World Council of Churches, get visas at the American Consulate. "Our aim is to give refugees a pleasant place to live, good or at least, decent food and clean rooms. The situation in most lagers is pretty terrible." Three camps were organized: Ranzenbach, Gugging, and Meidling. Glenn Good and John De Camp were in charge of immigration services for the other two camps so we met for discussions periodically. Carl Hurst worked with a team from the World Council of Churches. This team visited large camps and found Protestant families. (We took in more than Protestants and we worked with Catholic World Service and Lutheran World Service.) We also sent refugees to U.S., Canada, England, Australia, Dominican Republic, and many other countries. As time went on, each country would change the rules on how many and who would be acceptable or not acceptable for health, security, and new quota reasons. The average refugee in our camp stayed from 2-5 months because immigration became very difficult.

We also worked with ICEM (International Commission for European Migration) and other organizations. My job was basically to pick up refugees selected by WCC from crowded camps, bring them to our camp; then help them to find sponsoring organizations to help with travel and help them to immigrate. Our camp provided mostly individual rooms for families, fed them fairly well, provided recreation, worship services, counseling, encouragement, lent listening ears to their stories, held babies, etc.

Dwight Wiebe was in charge of operations in Vienna at first. We also worked out of the unit at Karlsschule where Mast Stolzfus was unit director. Early in January J. N. Byler came to Austria to be the Austrian director for 3 months. (An aside. I don't think he had much confidence in the Paxers, was relatively ill informed about what was going on in general. I can't honestly say what he did, if anything. But don't quote me on this.) I believe Byler worked with Milton Harder and Irene Bishop on refugee services. I get the impression that Wiebe went back to Germany and had perhaps less direct direction of the Vienna program.

4. By early June our camps were closed down. We found decent lodging for the remaining refugees. The major need for our camps was past and I assume other agencies were doing the job that needed doing. Hence, the refugee program with Paxers lasted about 6 months total. J.P. Duerksen was around at times and we had a men's choir that sang in many of the refugee camps in and around Vienna. I left Vienna in early June—drove the old Opel truck (max 60 kms. p. h.) from Vienna to Frankfurt/Main.

5. June 22-July 11, I was back at the building unit in Bechterdiessen. July 15 Wiebe invited me to be his secretary (Pax Secretary) since Orville Schmidt was going to MVS in Moscow for a month. I had several days with Orville in the Kaiserslautern office before he left. (The month however turned into 10 months as Pax Secretary). The office soon moved to Enkenbach. (I believe this was about the time Wiebe got married and he lived in an Enkenbach house). The office stayed there until the end of Wiebe's service as director and under the new director, Ray Kauffman until early February 1958 when we moved to Frankfurt where Peter Dyck was European Director.

6. I returned home by ship mid June 1958.

Bill Maust

Appendix F

Pax Study Report [5]

A. The Pax program has been making a unique and valuable contribution in the relief and mission outreach. Our churches and our young men continue to have a strong interest in this service and new opportunities for service should be sought.

B. Assignments are best in groups of five or more. Isolated assignments of one or two men in non-MCC or non-mission projects are not desirable. The ideal situation is where there is a unit leader, a matron, and regular pastoral supervision. These units make it possible to support a matron and unit leader from Pax contributions. When Pax men are serving in relief and mission projects the relief or mission group should be able to provide them with such help.

C. Most of the Pax men do best in manual or demonstration type work. Few have sufficient experience and training for teaching and administration.

D. There should be a general shift in program from Europe to areas in Eastern Europe, the Middle East, Africa, the Far East, and South America. A strong core of Pax men should remain in Europe but additional men should move into more underdeveloped areas. Possibilities for service would include agricultural units such as we have in Greece, assistance in road building work such as the Pax units are doing in Peru and Paraguay, and assistance in health.

E. Because the Pax financial arrangement provides no money for project expenses possibilities should be explored for Pax men to serve with Christian organizations as in Nepal. In such seconding relationships organizational and support lines musts be clear to retain the identity of our Pax men and their witness on the field. In these relationships we should also be sure that the men have good local leadership and spiritual care.

Respectfully submitted,
William T. Snyder
Robert W. Miller

Appendix G

Brief Pax-Related Biographies of Peachey and Redekop

Paul Peachey was deeply engaged in the early thinking and work promoting the Pax idea. Peachey's ancestry was the Swiss-Anabaptist branch, which began migrating to America in 1683. Because of religious persecution, Peachey's father grew up Amish in the Big Valley of Mifflin County, Pennsylvania, while his mother grew up in the Conservative Amish Mennonite Conference. Shem joined the Conservative Amish Mennonite conference. Paul joined the Old Mennonite Church during his student years at Eastern Mennonite College.

Peachey, newly married, had volunteered for several years beginning in January 1946, to serve in the relief unit in Belgium (described above in Chapter 1). Given the destruction in Europe, MCC was not yet sending married couples, so his wife, Ellen, joined him a year later as matron at the Brussel center. In the fall of 1947 they were transferred together to the MCC material aid program in the French Zone of Germany. After a brief furlough in summer 1948, they signed on for an extended term in an emerging post-material aid program in Germany, now that the economic crisis was easing. They were sent to Frankfurt am Main to develop a center and program for such activities—conferences, student and other exchanges, international voluntary work camps, etc. They remained in charge of the Frankfurt center, until the fall of 1951, when they left for Zurich for Paul to continue graduate study. Peachey had directed the MCC voluntary service work during 1948 (described in Chapter 3) and worked with Redekop in promoting the Pax idea. Peachy has long worked in various church agencies and has provided important visionary leadership throughout his life.

Calvin W. Redekop's socialization into the Mennonite heritage at Mountain Lake, Minnesota, as a member of the Evangelical Mennonite Brethren Church was sadly lacking, and is typical of young people in many communities. For a very representative example see the story of

Lynn Liechty of Berne, Indiana, as told in Perry Bush, *Two Kingdoms, Two Loyalties: Mennonite Pacifism in Modern America* (Baltimore: Johns Hopkins University Press, 1998), 1-5. In 1943, he was called by the draft board, and signed on as a 1A—regular military service. A physical disability prevented him from serving in the military. During his student days at Goshen College beginning in 1946, Redekop was introduced to the Anabaptist reformation and became committed to living up to the ideals of this heritage, and making up for lost time. He volunteered for service with the Mennonite Central Committee (MCC), which already at that time expressed the consummate idealism of many young Mennonites in the summer of 1949.[6]

Redekop arrived in Europe in early January 1950, not emotionally prepared to assimilate the devastation everywhere. The horrible destruction of what obviously had been rich historic culture, including the picturesque, romantic villages and towns, the elegant and historic cities, and majestic cathedrals was something of which no one could make sense. He will never forget the visit to Darmstadt, just south of Frankfurt soon after his arrival. Here one could see from one end of the city to the other end, with the unending piles of rubble not high enough to obstruct the view. The context of war and its consequences provided great stimulation to do something constructive.

Notes

Author's Preface

1. "Glory be to God on high, and on earth peace to men of good will," from the Latin Mass.

2. Actually only nineteen men and the Pax pastor, A. Lloyd Swartzentruber. Arnold Roth arrived several weeks later because all of his travel arrangements could not be made in time.

3. Peter Neufeld, Personal Diary, 1951, 1.

4. Ibid., 2.

5. Urie Bender, *Soldiers of Compassion* (Scottdale, Pa.: Herald Press, 1969), presents a major early source of the Pax story. The present account relies partly on the author's personal experiences in the early history, expanded in Appendix G. The author's own experience helps to contextualize the Pax story along with an attempt to present an objective account. The term *Pax boy* was widely used in an informal affectionate way, especially in Germany.

6. Wilbur Bontrager stated, "Roasted caterpillars took a little getting used to, But really, they're not bad" (Urie Bender, *Soldiers of Compassion,* 1969), 196. Jon Snyder's co-worker Dr. Paul Carlson was shot and killed by the Simbas in the house where they were hiding (Bender, 195).

7. Bender, *Soldiers of Compassion,* 10.

Chapter 1

1. "Pax boys" was an early designation, especially by the local German folk, who felt the "boys" were very young for the service they were performing. Pax was first referred to as the Danziger Builders Unit (Executive Committee Minutes, September 2, 1950). Later it was called Pax Services.

2. The expression and hence documentation of subjective emotions and feelings is not an extensive trait among Mennonites generally so it could not be expected among Pax men.

3. Peter Neufeld Diary, 3.

4. Builders Unit, which later became Pax Services. "In response to this resolution Executive Secretary Orie O. Miller presented a proposal to set up a separate program of service for IV-E men to be called 'Pax Services.'" (Executive Committee Minutes, March 17, 1951).

5. *Pax* is the Latin term for Peace. Urie Bender suggests Orie Miller first thought of the term Pax for the movement. "I tried to think of a word that would symbolize the idea these fellows were putting into practice. The Latin word for peace—Pax—came to me. The committee approved it and Pax was born" (*Soldiers of Compassion*, 266-267). Of course many other people had thought about the concept and the birth of Pax. The program, officially terminated in 1975, ended practically in 1976 when the last Pax man fulfilled his two years.

6. See "Reconstruction Work in France," *Mennonite Encyclopedia* 4, 262-263, for a full account. Mennonites did not have a foreign relief and service organization until 1919. Since no alternative service program existed during World War I, the AFSC work did not qualify as a substitute for military service but a "furlough" law was passed by Congress which allowed these men to carry out their full two years of work in France (262).

7. Mennonite Central Committee (MCC), founded in 1920, is the relief and service arm of the cooperating Mennonite conferences and denominations.

8. John Howard Yoder, "France," *Mennonite Encyclopedia* 2, 362.

9. Harold S. Bender, "Belgium," *Mennonite Encyclopedia* 1, 271-272.

10. There are numerous sources for the development of the international voluntary service movement. See Chapter 8. One source focuses on the Peace Corps, but has a good review of IVS, namely Roy Hoopes, *The Complete Peace Corps Guide* (New York: The Dial Press, 1961); another is Gerald T. Rice, *The Bold Experiment: JFK's Peace Corps* (Notre Dame: University of Notre Dame Press, 1985).

11. Ceresole served intermittent prison terms for refusing to pay the tax to exempt him from military service; Harold Josephson, ed., *Biographical Dictionary of Modern Peace Leaders* (Westport, Conn.: Greenwood Press, 1985).

12. Ibid., 150.

13. John D. Thiessen, *Mennonite and Nazi?* (Kitchener: Pandora Press, 1999), 91-92.

14. Lowell Detweiler, *The Hammer Rings Hope* (Scottdale, Pa.: Herald Press, 2000), 20.

Chapter 2

1. One cannot help but think that this reflects an idealism similar to the motivations for volunteering for the Peace Corps a decade later.

2. H. S. Bender. "Voluntary Service," *Mennonite Encyclopedia* 4, *848.* For a broad survey of the various Mennonite groups' involvement in VS, see Harold Penner, "Voluntary Service," *Mennonite Encyclopedia* 5, 917-918.

3. H. S. Bender, 849.

4. After describing the positive aspects of the CPS program, Melvin Gingerich states, "On the other hand, the CPS program revealed certain weaknesses. Many COs had a superficial understanding of their position and had little depth of spiritual experience. Intolerance and lack of love for each other led to tensions among campers. Working without pay and sometimes on jobs that appeared insignificant had a demoralizing

effect on many men. Some who witnessed government red tape and in-efficiency in certain areas reacted by developing cynicism and a lack of co-operation toward government." "Civilian Public Service," *Mennonite Encyclopedia* 1, 611. For an MCC-sponsored historical overview and eval-uation of Civilian Public Service (CPS), see "Civilian Public Service" in John Unruh, *In the Name of Christ* (Scottdale, Pa.: Herald Press, 1952). For an extended account of CPS, see the work of Pax man Albert Keim, *The CPS Story: An Illustrated History of Civilian Public Service* (Intercourse, Pa., Good Books, 1990).

5. In addition to the aspects described above, the student volunteer movement had also created great enthusiasm and interests already in the 1930s for developing international visits and exchanges among youth of many nations.

6. Unruh, 300.

7. Ibid.

8. Ibid., 301. The accounts of the wide variety of group experiences in the numerous work camps is not fully documented, but a number of camp diaries exist which give glimpses of the fabulously rich and excit-ing experiences many camps provided. Clearly only those who partici-pated in these camps will remember the stimulating times.

9. Ibid., 301.

10. For a brief account, see Unruh, "European Voluntary Service," in *In the Name of Christ*, 294-309.

11. Ibid. See also Melvin Gingerich, "Council of Mennonite and Affili-ated Colleges," *Mennonite Encyclopedia* 1, 722-723.

12. This is described below.

13. In 1951 at the MVS camp in Mainz, Germany, which the author personally directed, there were young people from eight different coun-tries, including two girls who had come surreptitiously and illegally from East Germany, and who were not sure they could return. Their presence provided an added measure of excitement and relevance to the camp ex-perience.

14. One of the most sensitive issues in the relationships between the European and American Mennonites was the issue of nonresistance. The former had generally relinquished the principle for a variety of reasons, while the latter had managed to maintain it, though for some time even in America, the peace position seemed to be hanging on precariously. For a review of the status of the nonresistant principle in both Europe and America, see "Nonresistance," in *Mennonite Encyclopedia* 3, especially 900-902.

15. A full published story of MVS which emerged in Europe is not yet available. For a brief review, see "Voluntary Service," in *Mennonite Ency-clopedia* 4, 848-849, and 5, 917-918; and "Mennonitscher Freiwiligendi-enst," *Mennonite Encyclopedia* 4, 649. These articles are general accounts of the voluntary service movement since World War II and do not give much specific information on the emergence of MVS.

16. The representatives were appointed by the respective groups and represent one of the few joint cooperative efforts among the four country

churches at that time.

17. Richard Hertzler, "Mennonitischer Freiwilligendienst," *Mennonite Encyclopedia* 3, 649. For a brief review of MVS activities, among them all the work camps staged until July 1952, including the Pax projects, see Calvin W. Redekop, "European Mennonite Voluntary Service," *Mennonite Life* (July 1952): 106-108.

18. There is probably no central archive where the records of all the projects are maintained. For a brief history of MVS, see Richard Hertzler, "Mennonitischer Freiwilligendienst," *Mennonite Encyclopedia* 3, 649. Calvin Redekop was director of both MFD/MVS as well as the Pax program from mid-1950 until he returned to the United States in December 1952.

19. The author remembers interminable evening camp discussions in which German young people defending Hitler, hammered home one point upon which Americans also had to agree, namely that he tried to destroy communism.

20. As a matter of fact, the number of nationalities present and languages spoken provided for almost continuing wonderfully humorous events and exasperating situations, at times.

21. Emily Brunk, *Espelkamp: The Mennonite Central Committee Shares in Community Building in a New Settlement for German Refugees* (Karlsruhe: Heinrich Schneider, 1951), 16. This account provides very significant background for the history of Espelkamp, which has achieved international renown as a model refugee resettlement city.

22. Ibid., 24.

23. "Espelkamp," *Mennonite Encyclopedia* 2, 249.

Chapter 3

1. In July 1950, North Korea had invaded South Korea, and the United States had re-introduced the draft to equip the military assistance to South Korea. The pervasiveness of the uneasiness because of the Korean conflict is indicated by the following minute of the MCC executive committee meeting in Basel, Switzerland, on August 12, 1950: "Decided that Paul Peachey and C. F. Klassen check with appropriate U.S. Military authorities in Europe on (a) our workers' CO status in Europe, and (b) American evacuation plans in event of military disturbance, and report to Akron with any recommendations." MCC files, IX 5-1-MCC.

2. Letter to J. N. Byler, September 5, 1950, MCC files, IC-19-3, Box 4.

3. As indicated below, the German government stipulation that the refugees supply up to ten percent of the cost of the housing was possible only by labor for the refugees were penniless. And further, this self help labor could only be applied if an outside agency such as MCC provided the initial resources to launch the construction, which included technical help in the form of the proposed American builders unit, Pax men.

4. Redekop letter to Miller, November 24, 1950, IX-19-3, box 4, file 69. The MCC executive secretary Miller and assistant secretary William T. Snyder were not totally in tune with Peachey and Redekop's concept of international reconstruction teams including American draftees and the

European Mennonites. For further discussion see Chapter 4, pages 50-53, and Notes.

5. Letter, December 4, 1950, MCC files, Germany, IX-6-3-47,

6. Ibid.

7. Minutes, MCC Executive Committee, December 2, 1950. See also C. J. Dyck, et. al., *Responding to Worldwide Needs* (Scottdale, Pa.: Herald Press, 1980), 135.

8. As indicated earlier, almost universally the Pax volunteers were affectionately referred to as "Pax boys" in Europe. This did not necessarily imply any denigration of their status as men but their youth. Clearly if nineteen-year-olds are deemed old enough to give their lives for their country, they should be given mature standing. Hence in this discussion even though they were referred to as boys, we will often speak of *men*.

9. Other countries of course were in dire straits as well, such as Austria, France, Greece, Holland, and Italy. But Germany was the most dramatic case, being almost totally destroyed. Appropriately Pax men served in all these countries, but were concentrated in Germany.

10. William Snyder to O. O. Miller, August 9, 1950, MCC Papers, IX-6-3-43, Archives of the Mennonite Church, Goshen, Ind.

11. Letter, September 25, 1950, IX-6-3-43.

12. MCC Executive Committee minutes, December 2, 1950, IX-5-1-MCC. C. F. Klassen was executive committee member of MCC and stationed in Europe to oversee the transporting and resettlement of Mennonite refugees

13. Letter, August 24, 1950, IX-6-3-43.

14. See Appendix B, "Alternative Service," for a concise statement on these developments.

15. "Memorandum," MCC, Basel, Switzerland, March 29, 1951. Blocked funds were German funds retained in foreign banks, including the Swiss, during the war, and released to various institutions after the war upon the approval of the German Government for use in German reconstruction.

16. For an extensive explication of the intricacies of one such building project, see Horst Klaassen's description of the arrangements for the Backnang project, including specific costs and contributions of the refugees and the Pax men. "Bau der Mennonitensiedlung," in *Die Backnanger Mennoniten* (Backnang: Mennonitengemeinde Backnang, 1976).

17. In Germany, forestry regulations forbade the cutting down of any trees without county or state approval.

18. The Dodge Power Wagon was one of the vehicles MCC loaned to the Pax program and it served well for many years in many jobs. For an excellent first hand account of the beginning of the Espelkamp MVS/Pax operation, including a picture of the Dodge Power wagon pulling down trees, see Milton Harder, director of the Espelkamp unit, " 'Die Mennoniten' at Espelkamp." *Mennonite Life* (July 1952): 109-110.

19. Neufeld, Diary, 3. In *Soldiers of Compassion*, 26, Bender indicates that it was Dwight Weibe who gave the orders. This is obviously wrong. Wiebe, the third Pax director, did not arrive in Europe until 1954.

20. For one of the most extensive accounts of a building project from beginning to end, including the story of the refugees that were settled, see the story of the Backnang project, described in Horst Klaassen, *Die Backnanger Mennoniten.*

21. Gerhard Ratzlaff, *Die Ruta Transchao: wie sie entstand* (Asuncion: Self published 1998). The book includes a marvelous pictorial review of the project, unit life, and activities of the Pax men. Doubtless this project in many ways could be described as an expedition to a romantic frontier, but the hot summer tempers this view somewhat.

22. Urie Bender, 161-162.

23. Ibid., 164.

Chapter 4

1. Paul Toews, *Mennonites in American Society, 1930-1970* (Scottdale, Pa.: Herald Press, 1996), 213.

2. Urie Bender, 24.

3. Ibid., 222.

4. Unruh, 280. For a succinct account of the draft and alternative service, see Appendix B, "Alternative Service."

5. Victor Olson, "Selective Service Reviews the I-W Program," *Mennonite Life* (July, 1958): 99.

6. Ibid., 99. See Appendix B for I-W definition. In addition, for an extensive description of the I-W program, see Dirk W. Eitzen and Timothy R. Falb, "An Overview of the Mennonite I-W Program," *Mennonite Quarterly Review* 56, no. 4 (October 1982): 365-381.

7. "The NSBRO was to serve as the liaison between the churches and other groups and the National Selective Service office," says "National Service Board for Religious Objectors," *Mennonite Encyclopedia* 3, 814.

8. Henry A. Fast letter, August 1, 1951, to A. Lloyd Swartzentruber. MCC files, IX-19-3, Box 5.

9. There is a considerable irony in Hershey's role. A third generation Mennonite four star general, he was well situated to understand the Mennonite beliefs and intentions.

10. Letter, July 31, 1952, MCC files, IX-19-5, Pax Misc.

11. Electronic mail from James Juhnke, July 21, 2000, Peter Dyck letter to William T. Snider, November 9, 1959, MCC Files, IX-19-4.

12. Ibid., Dyck letter.

13. Garber, 53.

14. Harry E. Martens, in *The Mennonite* (July 13, 1954).

15. Jake and Jane Friesen, "Pax: A History of MCC Pax and its Services," in Wilfred Unruh, *A Study of Mennonite Service Programs* (Elkhart, Ind.: Institute of Mennonite Studies, 1965).

16. A-77. See also Appendix C, "The Aims of the Pax Program."

17. The group, originally referred to as the "Danziger Builder's Unit" was under executive director of MCC direction, but administered via the Relief Section of MCC, with the field operations channeled through the European MCC director at Basel, Switzerland, and finally under the direction of the International Voluntary Service program director in Eu-

rope headquartered at first in Frankfurt, Germany. MCC files, "Memorandum," March 29, 1951, IX-19-3, box 5. See Appendix D for flow chart of decision making.

18. Bob Miller, in Friesen, p. A-279. The organization chart of the Pax program defies understanding. See Appendix D. Pax would not have worked had it not been for the informal trust that existed throughout the MCC and the supporting constituencies.

19. Memorandum, Thursday, March 29, 1951. Present: C. F. Klassen, Harold Buller, J. N. Byler, Henry Loewen, Paul Peachey, C. L. Graber, and Cal Redekop," MCC files, IX-19-3, box 5.

20. Letter, April 9, 1952 MCC files IX-6-3-59. All the letters from Redekop pertaining to Pax were written on the new "Mennonite Voluntary Service: An International Organization for Christian Service" stationery.

21. As a younger worker Redekop, not eager to work in a context of a dissatisfied and disapproving superior, replied on April 16, "I feel I owe an apology to Bro. Snyder and you for the tone of my letter concerning the [relations] of Pax Projects and relations to MVS. I was probably a little too impatient in my approach." Letter, April 16, 1952, MCC files, IX-6-3-59.

22. It is clear that one of the major concerns was the responsibility MCC felt for the supervision and effectiveness of the young "boys." On August 14, 1951, A. Lloyd Swartzentruber, Pax pastor wrote to William T. Snyder, "I spoke to the boys about your concern especially that they are quite young. They all said they would be quite careful and I believe they will [regarding vacation plans]. When I wrote you before, I said that no problem had arisen that had not been anticipated." (IX-19-3, MCC, Europe). Almost a year later, Pax Pastor Jesse Short expressed a similar concern, "I am convinced that there needs to be two camps—a VS and a Pax. In order to keep our testimony aglow, better care must be taken in selecting young people for VS. Some come here thinking it will be a summer resort—work when they want to and if they are too tired in the morning they just stay in and sleep. In the evening they go out to the dance, shows, smoke, and come in any time they want to." (IX-19-5).

23. IX-19-5, 1952, "Pax Misc."

24. With the exception of Greece, which was sufficiently organically related that there was conscious awareness of relationship.

Chapter 5

1. Emily Brunk, *Espelkamp*, 10.

2. Letter, April 10, 1951.

3. Ibid., 12.

4. There is an area along the Rhine that has a deep layer of volcanic ash which produces a very usable material for building blocks.

5. See Table 2 for fuller statistics on the major Pax projects.

6. Curtis Janzen, "Our Pax Boys in Europe," *Mennonite Life* (April 1954): 80-82.

7. Urie Bender, 27.

8. Friesen and Friesen, A-293.

9. *Euro Pax News* 1, no. 1 (September 1954): 1.

10. Merlin Garber, *Karlsschule*, 18. A bilingual plaque commemorating the work of the Pax/BVS unit was dedicated there on May 5, 2001. Garber's history of the unit is very helpful in describing how the project emerged, and offers insightful perspective interpersonal unit dynamics, and relationship to the community. Unfortunately, the book is no longer in print.

11. MCC Executive Committee Minutes, May 11, 1957. A total of 180,000 refuges had entered Austria and more than 131,404 had emigrated to new homes. The minutes do not indicate how many were helped by the Pax operated camps.

12. Urie Bender, 135. STICA was the Paraguayan counterpart of the U.S. Point Four program.

13. Gerhard Ratzlaff, *Die Ruta Transchaco*, 188-9.

14. See R. L. Hartzler, "Mennonite Cooperation in the Congo Inland Mission," *Mennonite Life* (April, 1961), 88, for an account of the mission program, including the names of Pax men who served in the mission program. See also John Janzen,"Pax Work in Congo," in the same issue.

15. "Appendix I Paxmen According to Country" in Bender, *Soldiers of Compassion. Reaching the Other Side*, by Paxer Earl Martin, describes his experience in Vietnam.

16. For a first hand account of the Bolivia program, see the account by Harley Showalter at the end of Chapter 7.

17. This list includes only the countries with Pax units of more than 2-3 persons per project. Individual Pax men served in numerous countries for a variety of projects and times.

18. The number indicates how many countries Pax was involved in that year, followed by the names of the countries, followed by the countries where projects were terminated.

19. The total countries served minus the ones terminated do not necessarily add up because some projects were dormant at times and because of the lack of complete information.

20. The information on project closings was more difficult to obtain as they became part of MCC programs.

21. *The 1990 Almanac* (New York: Houghton Mifflin, 1990), 129.

22. About sixteen percent served for three years. It would be very interesting to discover the reasons for this "extra mile."

23. MCC Executive Committee minutes, December 10-11, 1975, 19.

24. Ibid., Personnel Appointments, 2. With the term being normally for two years, we can establish that the Pax program ended officially in 1976.

25. Termination dates have been difficult to establish.

26. Only the larger projects with extensive information are listed here. The most general survey of the early European Pax projects is found in *Euro Pax News* (July 1958), and Bender's *Soldiers* provides useful information. Appendix 1 provides a tabular account of the countries in which Pax men were stationed, how many, and the dates, until 1968. An accurate account of the total program would require a massive amount of re-

search time in the MCC records located in the archives of the Mennonite Church at Goshen College. The total program is clearly in need of accurate documentation.

27. *Eirene* means "peace" in Greek, and for International Christian Service for Peace, an organization sponsored by the historic peace churches consisting of the Church of the Brethren and Mennonites. See H. S. Bender, "Pax," *Mennonite Encyclopedia, 129.*

28. One obvious reason why Pax was such a flexible and responsive entity was that Pax men were not married and could be shifted almost instantly. This factor has not received any attention as far as the author knows.

29. *MCC Annual Report.* 83. The author is not identified, but the MCC executive secretary is responsible for the contents.

30. Richard Yoder, Calvin Redekop, and Vernon Jantzi, *The Anabaptist-Mennonite Experience in Development*, (manuscript in process, 2001), 6.

31. Henry Rempel, "Development Work," *Mennonite Encyclopedia* 5, 229.

32. The only valid explanation seems to be that Rempel was not aware or informed of the Pax efforts. The editors of *Mennonite Encyclopedia* should, however, have noted the lacuna.

33. For example, Harold Miller and Fremont Regier have spent much of their lives in Africa. It is unfair to give examples because other worthy persons are excluded. This only accentuates the need for a thorough research on the role ex-Pax men played in development work.

Chapter 6

1. The men serving in some of these so-called exotic places probably will disagree, since most of these projects were rather isolated and primitive.

2. "Minutes," MCC Executive Committee, December 2, 1950, 9.

3. Redekop, as a member of the Frankfurt MCC unit, reported to Paul Peachey, Germany director for a variety of activities involving his role as an MCC worker. Since C.F. Klassen was a member of the executive committee and resident in Frankfurt, Redekop also reported to Klassen who was head of the refugee resettlement program, regarding issues which involved Pax. However the European office of MCC was also in the chain of command, and many decisions were cleared through that office often without consulting the Pax director. Further since the Relief office in Akron was responsible for the voluntary service and relief activities, many actions were routed through that section. And finally, since the executive secretary's office was the ultimate location for responsibility, most issues finally ended up in that office and decisions were often unilaterally handed back to the Pax director.

To complicate matters Redekop was also director of the European Mennonite Voluntary Service (MVS) program until December 1952. The intimate inter-connections between the two programs has been discussed above. The Akron office also communicated with the Basel European office regarding Pax matters, often circumventing the Frankfort Pax office on a variety of issues by arranging details directly with the Akron office.

While a realistic reason may have been the incompetence of the first Pax director, it is also possible it was the experimental and multi-faceted nature of the Pax program which developed into a typical MCC administrative hodgepodge. In fact the *Pax Handbook* referred to above states that except for Europe, the Pax program will be directed on a case-by-case basis.

In this connection it has been said that the MCC is such a convoluted organization that by all logic it should not have been able to function. Beyond that, the experimental nature of the program, composed of young boys (as they were called) increased the protectiveness of the home office. As the program matured, especially under Dwight Wiebe's leadership, the organizational structure became much more rationalized even though differences of perspective continued.

For an analysis of MCC as an organization, see my "The Mennonite Central Committee Story," especially 99-103. *Mennonite Quarterly Review* 67, no. 1 (January 1993): 84-103, and my "The 'MCC Ethos' and the Organizational Revolution," *Mennonite Quarterly Review* 70, no. 1 (January 1996): 107-132. See Appendix D for diagram.

4. Eirene, Greek word for peace, was also known as "International Christian Service for Peace," sponsored jointly by MCC, Brethren Service Commission, and the German Mennonites with contributions received from other sources, especially the World Council of Churches. (*MCC Annual Reports, 1960*, A-4). The report continues, "Near Oujda on a large farm some 70 Algerian refugee men and boys are cared for. United Nations is providing the maintenance and Eirene personnel is attempting to give vocational training. Eirene is headquartered in Kaiserslautern, Germany. MCC contributed $7,000 in 1960."

5. *Euro Pax News* (September 1954): 4, and Orville Schmidt letter, January 22, 2000.

6. In a letter to William Snyder on June 16, 1951, Swartzentruber stated, "The fellows [Pax] know the VS and Relief [MCC appointed personnel] workers time of service and the allowances they are given during the vacation period. It is my opinion that it would be the best to follow the same pattern as is followed in other [MCC] units."

7. Letter from William T. Snyder to Swartzentruber, March 15, 1951.

8. William Snyder to Swartzenruber, May 10, 1951.

9. Snyder letter to Swartzentruber, May 10, 1951. The grading system was subsequently discontinued.

10. Letter to Snyder, n.d. probably early May 1951.

11. Letter, November 30, 1995.

12. Gerhard Ratzlaff, *Die Ruta Transchaco,* 168-190. Pages 188-89 include the names of all the men that served, totaling 29. The list also includes ten men from Menno, Fernheim, and Neuland in the Chaco and Bergthal, east Paraguay, who served alongside the Pax men. See page 170 for a picture of the Harry Harder family, and page 174 for a picture of the Pax unit at dinner.

13. Merlin Garber, *Karlsschule,* 28.

14. Orville Schmidt letter to Hannalora Bergen, January 17, 2000.

15. Unfortunately there is no official MCC listing of matrons who served Pax so it is not a definitive list. These women also were often loaned to other MCC projects for a specified time.

16. MVS and its activities related to Pax will be described below.

17. Unpublished interview, from files of Gerhard Ratzlaff, in author's files.

18. Menno Wiebe Memorandum: "MCC Participation in the Trans Chaco Highway Construction," February 28, 1997, in author's files. A translated version of this memorandum appears in Ratzlaff's book.

19. Neufeld, Diary, 5.

20. "Sparky," not his real nickname, was from eastern Pennsylvania and had a great reputation for humorous tricks and stunts. The author, having spent the previous night at the unit was never told that this event was planned, and was as surprised as the rest.

21. Every Pax reunion of the first group, and there have been many, recounts this event along with others of "Sparky" with peals of laughter and glee. The commentary usually includes the observations that it expressed Pax men's protest to their inferior status, but on the other hand also that Mennonite officialdom, was after all human and recognized their common humanity.

22. Neufeld, Diary, 5.

23. *Euro Pax News* (April 1956).

24. Ibid., 3. See also Urie Bender, 29-32 for an extended description of unit life.

25. Urie Bender, 30.

26. Garber, 25.

27. Letter, September 18, 2000.

28. No reasons for its demise are available, but it appears the European projects were leveling off. *Euro Pax News* illustrates the degree to which an esprit de corps had developed in the European setting, not matched in other areas, obviously because units in other countries lacked the critical mass. The newspaper provides some useful insights into the spirit and ethos in which the Pax men worked and lived.

29. Urie Bender, 48.

30. Carl R. Jantzen, "Ye have done it unto me," *Mennonite Life* (January 1957): 35-38. Jantzen provides a helpful brief history of IVS, which will be useful in the discussion of Pax world impact. "Snyder told me about IVS. It had been felt by a number of public-spirited citizens, judging from the experiences of MCC, Brethren Service Commission, American Friends Service Committee, and others, that voluntary agency efforts sometimes give a needed emphasis to the personal or human interest one people may have for another. IVS was set up as a private, non-profit agency to tasks that government people have not been able to do successfully. So a contract was signed with the Technical Cooperation Administration, Point Four's label in 1953, to work with Point Four of Iraq. This was the first government contract for IVS, although a couple of fellows had already been sent to Egypt under sponsorship of World Neighbors," 35.

31. Ibid., 37. Interestingly Jantzen does not refer to Pax at all, but rather to MCC and IVS in his story, which suggests that the "Pax" ethos so strong in larger units, such as Germany, Greece, and Paraguay, was not as pronounced in this "ecumenically" structured unit in a far-away place. It is clear that the IVS unit provided a dramatic expansion of cross-cultural experience for the Pax men, and Iraq was a pronounced example.

32. For a detailed report on MVS activities from 1948-1952, see Calvin W. Redekop, "European Mennonite Voluntary Service," *Mennonite Life* (July 1952): 106-108. The table on page 108 lists twenty-three work camp projects that had been conducted, in which 218 American (including Pax men) and 379 youth from ten nations volunteered and worked together. Some eight years later, The "MCC Annual Report " reports, "During 1960 MVS conducted 17 work camps running from three to six weeks, with 313 volunteers, of which 43 percent were Mennonites. The idea of MVS is slowly gaining support among the European Mennonites. LaMarr Reichert, executive secretary of MVS, says, "Many church leaders who three or four years ago were very much against exposing their young people to the world now support MVS strongly,' " A-5. For additional information and bibliography, see Harold Penner, "Voluntary Service."

33. Richard Rush, Diary, 5.

34. Rush, Diary, 8. Gronau was the MCC refugee processing center through which most refugees went on their way to new homes in North and South America. See John D. Unruh, "Gronau," 189-191.

35. A-8 The tension between the area Pax office in Germany and the Akron home office was alluded to above.

Chapter 7

1. Larry Kehler,"A Profile of Mennonite Personnel Involved in International Experience. *Proceedings of the Sixteenth Conference on Mennonite Educational and Cultural Problems,* (June 8-9, 1967), 34.

2. Fremont Regier, four page single-spaced eye witness report of the accident. Fremont was at the other end of the dugout when Larry disappeared. He and the others tried desperately to find him, but of no avail, e-mail report, May 24, 2000. The *MCC Annual Meeting Minutes*, December 27-28, state tersely, "As Larry was wading out to a small island to tie the boat he was caught in an unusual current. He was swept down the river, drowned, and his body was never recovered," 6.

3. John Bertsche, *CIM/AIM: A Story of Vison, Commitment and Grace* (np.nd. 1998), 144. For the dramatic story, see Bender, *Soldiers,* 185-196. See also Robert J. Decker, rector, *News from L'Universite Libre du Congo* (Leopoldville, Congo, 1964).

4. "VietNam," *Mennonite Encyclopedia* 5, 912. The author himself was implicated in a way, for as one of Gerber's professors, he encouraged him to consider Pax as a way of finding a direction and purpose in life.

5. Urie Bender's *Soldiers of Compassion* lists 674 men as of June 1968. The Pax Planning Committee has documented approximately 299 more men until the termination of Pax in 1975, which brings the total to around 1,180. Bender's book suggests they served an average of two and a half

years. If that estimate is correct, the men contributed at least 2,400 man-years. They worked in 409 plus countries, from Austria to Zambia, on the European, Asian, African, and South American continents.

6. C. J. Dyck, Robert Kreider, and John A. Lapp, *Responding to Worldwide Needs*, 136.

7. *Pax Handbook, 1952, 3*. See Appendix C for full text. Also Friesen and Friesen, A-277.

8. Exhibit 12, MCC Executive Committee Minutes, July 6, 1957.

9. Ibid., 3. This bit of information may provide considerable insight into the unusual motivation of the Pax men.

10. Ibid. 4.

11. Ibid., A-286. Sources other than Bender's are utilized to broaden the base of testimonials, but none supercede *Soldiers of Compassion.*

12. Ibid., A-297.

13. Ibid., A-314.

14. Kehler, 33.

15. That is to say, the Pax experience was a powerful shift in their horizons and outlook, but it also helped determine their future commitments, direction, and values.

16. Bender, 141-142.

17. Ibid., 88.

18. The phrase "was open to Pax men who had served in other areas" sound a bit strange, but resulted basically from the fact that the smaller Pax units did not have the mass typically needed to establish ongoing planning and activities.

19. *Gospel Herald* (October 5, 1961), 19. No information has come to light indicating what the dilemma was.

20. Ibid., 78-79. Backnang had received a major contingent of Mennonite refugees after the war. See John. D. Unruh, *In the Name of Christ*, 191ff.

21. This issue is addressed a bit more directly in Chapter 8.

22. In recent discussions with ex-Paxers by the author, the spirit of adventure and desire to see more of the world was strongly affirmed.

23. The fact that later volunteers generally had more education than the first ones indicates the changing times. As is generally known, the 1950s and 1960s were times of dramatic change in the United States; hence Pax men who left the United States mainland in the early 1950s were different from those who volunteered after the mid 1960s.

24. "M.C.C. Pax Services: A History and a Case Study," unpublished paper, Canadian Mennonite Bible College, 1989.

25. A mail survey conducted by the author, April, 2000.

26. Electronic mail, July 21, 2000, selected excerpts.

27. C. J. Dyck et al., *Responding to Worldwide Needs*, 123.

28. Ibid., 123.

Chapter 8

1. For an intensive overview of the changes in orientation toward the world, see Leo Driedger and Don Kraybill, *Mennonite Peacemaking: From*

Quietism to Activism (Scottdale, Pa.: Herald Press, 1994). For an in-depth analysis of the dramatic changes in the Mennonite Church during this period, see the biography of *Harold S. Bender,* by Al Keim .

2. Melvin Gingerich, "Civilian Public Service," *Mennonite Encyclopedia* 1, 611.

3. Perry Bush, *Two Kingdoms, Two Loyalties: Mennonite Pacifism in Modern America* (Baltimore: Johns Hopkins University Press, 1998), 30.

4. *Mennonite Life* (October 1961): 180.

5. Ibid., 181.

6. "Pax-Peace Through Love," *Mennonite Life* (July 1961): 104.

7. There are numerous accounts of the sources of the Peace Corps: Brent Ashabranner, *A Moment In History: The First Ten Years of the Peace Corps* (Garden City, N.Y.: Doubleday and Co., 1971.); Roy Hoopes, *The Complete Peace Corps Guide* (New York: The Dial Press, 1961); Gerald Ric T. Rice, *The Bold Experiment: JFK's Peace Corps* (Notre Dame: University of Notre Dame Press, 1985), and Charles G. Wingenbach, *The Peace Corps, Who, How and Why* (New York: The John Day Company, 1969).

8. Hoopes, 9. Fretz also mentions the James idea of a moral equivalent to war as a source of the Peace Corps idea.

9. Wingenbach, 17-18.

10. Brent Ashabranner, 12.

11. See Stuart Rawlings, ed., *The IVS Experience from Algeria to Vietnam* (Washington, D.C.: IVS, 1992).

12. Hoopes, 13. It is important in this context to note that William T. Snyder, assistant executive secretary, was a board member of IVS from its founding in 1963. It is obvious that his presence, reflecting the whole breadth of Mennonite thought and experience, was important in the formation of IVS and hence its influence on the Peace Corps.

13. IX-12-3, MCC Collection, Report Files, "Peace Corps" reprint of *Congressional Record* (August 24, 1961), 15871.

14. From its beginnings In 1951 to 1957.

15. Wingenbach, 21.

16. As indicated earlier, some Quaker young men served in MVS and Pax services.

17. Hoopes, 14.

18. Ibid., 14-15.

19. *Hearings before the Committee on Foreign Relations, United States Senate, Eighty Seventh Congress, S. 2000* (June 1961), 158-159.

20. Ibid., 159.

21. "Overseas Questionnaire," American Institute for Research, Washington. D.C., n.d.

22. Mennonite Central Committee Peace Corps Statement, November 2, 1961.

23. "Peace Corps Significance for Relief and Service Agencies," May 11-13, 1961.

24. Ibid., 2.

25. It appears that the Peace Corps approached the MCC about making a submission, for the Minutes of the conjoint meeting on May 11-13,

1961 include the comment, "The Peace Corps had taken initiative to ask MCC for information on the possibility of expanding its Haiti work with Peace Corps support."

26. These proposals are undated with no identification as to which office prepared them. It can be presumed that they were prepared by Kermit Derstine, serving in the Relief Section and with Pax, who wrote a memo on November 14, 1961, to Urban Peachey, head of the Personnel department regarding the problems of working with the Peace Corps.

27. Appendix B, "Peace Corps," X-12-4.

28. *MCC News Service* (October, 11, 1961).

29. James Juhnke, electronic mail, July 21, 2000.

30. Wolfgang Krauss and Ben Redekop, *The Difficulties of Being Peace Church* (Karlsruhe: Deutsches Mennonitisches Friedenskomitee, 1988).

31. It is interesting that Larry Miller, executive secretary of the Mennonite World Conference is proposing an international structure for providing all types of assistance to Mennonite congregations, as well as the communities in which they live. Miller states, "The immediate danger for the MWC (Mennonite World Conference) is not too much structure or centralization, but not being able to respond adequately to calls for its involvement [to the needs around the world]." Miller, cited in *Courier* 15, no. 2 (2000), 6.

Appendixes

1. There is no date or source for this document, but presumably it was prepared for the first unit.

2. *The Brethren Encyclopedia* (Philadelpia: The Brethren Encyclopedia Inc., 1983), 19. Reprinted by permission.

3. *Pax Handbook, 1952, 2.* There is no indication of who the writer was or when in 1952 it was published. Being produced before the program was hardly a year old. It is clear that it was used as an orientation tool and also as a recruitment device. The European staff had no awareness of, or hand in creating it. This goes for most of the other materials regarding Pax that were produced in Akron.

4. The introduction refers to a project operating in Bolivia which suggests it was produced during or after 1962.

5. Submitted to MCC executive committee, December 14, 1957.

6. MCC became a surrogate church for many young Mennonites, impatient with the traditionalism and narrow-mindedness of the rank and file congregations.

Pax 50 Bibliography

"Alternative Service." *The Brethren Encyclopedia* 1. Philadelphia: Brethren Encyclopedia, 1983, 19-20.

Ashabranner, Brent. *A Moment in History: The First Ten Years of the Peace Corps.* Garden City, N.Y.: Doubleday and Co., 1971.

Bender, H. S. "Pax." *Mennonite Encyclopedia* 4, 129.

———. "Voluntary Service." *Mennonite Encyclopedia* 4, 848-849.

———. "National Service Board for Religions Objectors." *Mennonite Encyclopedia* 4, 813-814.

———. "Belgium." *Mennonite Encyclopedia* 1, 271.

Bender, Urie. *Soldiers of Compassion.* Scottdale, Pa.: Herald Press, 1969.

Bergman, Gene. "An Evaluation of Foreign Service Experience." *Proceedings of the Eleventh Conference on Mennonite Educational and Cultural Problems,* 1967, 40-49.

Bertsche, John. *CIM/AIM: A Story of Vision, Commitment and Grace.* Elkhart: N.P., 1998.

Brunk, Emily. *Espelkamp: The Mennonite Central Committee Shares in Community Building in a New Settlement for German Refugees.* Karlsruhe, Germany: Heinrich Schneider, 1951.

Bush, Perry. *Two Kingdoms, Two Loyalties: Mennonite Pacifism in Modern America.* Baltimore: Johns Hopkins University Press, 1998.

Congressional Record: Senate. June 22-23, 1961.

Congressional Record: Senate. August 24, 1961.

Crous, Ernst. "Nonresistance." *Mennonite Encyclopedia* 3, 897-907.

Detweiler, Lowell. *The Hammer Rings Hope.* Scottdale, Pa.: Herald Press, 2000.

Driedger, Leo and Donald B. Kraybill. *Mennonite Peacemaking.* Scottdale, Pa.: Herald Press, 1994.

Dyck, C. J. *Responding to Worldwide Needs.* Scottdale, Pa.: Herald Press, 1980.

Eitzen, Dirk W. and Timothy R. Falb, "An Overview of the Mennonite I-W Program." *Mennonite Quarterly Review* 56, no. 4 (October 1982): 365-381.

Euro-Pax News. Frankfurt, Germany. 1954-1958.

Fretz, J. Winfield. "Peace Corps: Child of Historic Peace Churches." *Mennonite Life* 16, no. 4 (October 1964): 178-181.

Friesen, Jake and Jane. "Pax: A History of MCC Pax and its Services." in Wilfrid Unruh, *A Study of Mennonite Service Programs.*

Garber, Merlin. *Karlsschule.* Salem, Va.: Merlin Garber, 1983.

Gingerich, Melvin. "Civilian Public Service." *Mennonite Encyclopedia* 1, 604-611.

———. "Council of Mennonite and Affiliated Colleges." *Mennonite Encyclopedia* 1, 722-723.

Good, Phyllis Pellman. "Mennonite World Conference: Who Are We Now?" *Courier,* 6-13.

Harder, Milton. "Die Mennoniten at Espelkamp." *Mennonite Life* 7, no. 3 (July 1952): 109-110.

Hartzler, R. L. "Mennonite Cooperation in the Congo Inland Mission." *Mennonite Life* 16, no. 2 (April 1961): 70-75.

Hershberger, Guy F. "Reconstruction Work in France." *Mennonite Encyclopedia* 4, 262-163.

Hertzler, Richard. "Mennonitischer Freiwilligendiesnst." *Mennonite Encyclopedia 3, 649.*

Hoopes, Roy. *The Complete Peace Corps Guide.* New York: The Dial Press, 1961.

Janzen, John. "Pax Work in the Congo." *Mennonite Life* 16, no. 2 (April 1961): 96.

Janzen, Curt. "Our Pax Boys in Europe." *Mennonite Life* 9, no. 2 (April 1954): 80-82.

Josephson, Harold, ed. *Biographical Dictionary of Modern Peace Leaders.* Westport, Conn.: Greenwood Press, 1985.

Juhnke, James. "Pax-Peace through Love." *Mennonite Life* 15, no. 3 (July 1961): 102-104.

"Karlsschule." *The Brethren Encyclopedia,* 684.

Kasper, Arlo. "The I-W in Action." *Mennonite Life* 13, no. 3 (July 1958): 106-108, 120.

Kehler, Larry. "A Profile of Mennonite Personnel Involved in International Experience." *Proceedings of the eleventh Conference on Mennonite Educational and Cultural Problems.* 1967, 9-39.

Keim, Albert. *The CPS Story: An Illustrated Story of Civilian Public Service.* Intercourse. Pa.: Good Books, 1990.

———. "Alternative Service." in *Mennonite Encyclopedia* 5, 18-19.

———. *Harold S. Bender, 1897-1962.* Scottdale, Pa.: Herald Press, 1998.

Kennedy, John. *Executive Order: Establishment and Administration of the Peace Corps in the Department of State.* Washington D.C.: The White House, March 1, 1961.

Klassen, Doug. M.C.C. "Pax Services: A History and A Case Study." Unpublished paper, Canadian Mennonite Bible College, April 1989.

Klaassen, Horst. *Die Backnanger Mennoniten.* Backnang: Heinrich Schneider, 1976.

Krahn, Cornelius. "An Era of Reconstruction." *Mennonite Life* 10, no. 4 (October 1955): 151-172.

Kreider, Robert S. and Rachel Waltner Goosen. *The MCC Experience: Hungry, Thirsty, a Stranger.* Scottdale, Pa.: Herald Press, 1988.

Laszlo, Erwin and Jong Youl Yoo, eds. *World Encyclopedia of* Peace. Oxford: Pergamon Press, 1986.

Luce, Don, "IVS Yesterday and Today." In Stuart Rawlings, *The IVS Experience.*

Martens, Harry. "Our Youth in Christian Service." *Mennonite Life* 18, no. 2 (April 1952): 77-79.

Martin, Earl. *Reaching the Other Side.* New York: Crown Publishers, 1978.

MCC News Service. Akron: Mennonite Central Committee.

Mennonite Central Committee. *Annual Reports,* Archives of the Mennonite Church. Goshen, Ind.

Mennonite Central Committee files. Archives of the Mennonite Church, Goshen, Indiana. Includes all Executive Committee minutes, annual meeting minutes, etc.

Mennonite Encyclopedia, Vols. 1-5. Scottdale, Pa.: Herald Press, 1955, 1956, 1957, 1959, 1990.

Metzler, James. "Vietnam." *Mennonite Encyclopedia* 5, 911-913.

"Nationwide Pax Conference." *Gospel Herald* (October 3, 1961): 19.

Neufeld, Horst. *40 Jahre Mennoniten Gemeinde Expelkamp e.v.* Espelkamp: Mittwaldruck, 1993.

Olson, Victor. "Selective Service Reviews the I-W Program." *Mennonite Life* 13, no. 3 (July 1958): 99-100.

"Overseas Questionnaire." Washington, D.C.: American Institute for Research, n.d.

Paix: Pelle et Pioche: histoire du Service Civil Internationale de 1919-1954. Lausanne: Editions de Service Civil International, 1955.

Pax Handbook. Akron: MCC, 1952; 2nd. ed., 1962

PAX: European Services: 1957. Frankfurt: MCC-Pax, 1958.

Peachey, Paul. "Espelkamp." *Mennonite Encyclopedia* 2, 249.

Penner, Harold A. "Voluntary Service." *Mennonite Encyclopedia 5,* 917-918.

Ratzlaff, Gerhard. *Die Ruta Transchaco.* Asuncion: N.P., 1998.

Rawlings, Stuart, ed., *The IVS Experience from Algeria to Vietnam.* Washington D.C.: IVS, 1992.

Redekop, Calvin W. "The Pax Movement: A Small Contribution to the Peaceable Community." *Mennonite Life* 54, no. 12 (March 1999): 27-32.

———. "The Mennonite Central Committee and the Organizational Revolution." *Mennonite Quarterly Review* 70, no. 1 (January 1995): 107-132.

———. "The Mennonite Central Committee Story: A Review Essay." *Mennonite Quarterly Review* 67, no. 1 (January 1993): 84-103.

———. "European Mennonite Voluntary Service." *Mennonite Life* 7, no. 3 (July 1952): 106-108.

Rempel, Henry. "Development Work." *Mennonite Encyclopedia* 5, 228-231.

Rice, Gerald T. *The Bold Experiment: JFK's Peace Corps.* Notre Dame: Notre Dame University Press, 1985.

Sherk, J. Harold. "The Alternative Service Law and its Operation." *Mennonite Life* 13, no. 3 (July 1958): 103-105.

Snyder, William T. and Robert Miller, "Pax Study Report." in Dyck, *Responding to Worldwide Needs.*

"The Story Behind the Peace Corps." *Family Weekly* (April 30, 1961).

The Peace Corps: Hearings before the Committee on Foreign Relations, United States Senate, Eighty Seventh Congress, June 22 and 23, 1961.

The 1990 Almanac. New York: Houghton Mifflin, 1990, 129.

Thiesen, John D. *Mennonite and Nazi? Attitudes Among Mennonite Colonists in Latin America, 1933-1945.* Kitchener, Ont.: Pandora Press, 1999.

Toews, Paul. *Mennonites in American Society.* Scottdale, Pa.: Herald Press, 1996.

Unruh, Wilfrid. *A Study of Mennonite Service Programs.* Elkhart, Ind.: Institute of Mennonite Studies, 1965.

Unruh, John D. *In the Name of Christ.* Scottdale, Pa.: Herald Press, 1952.

Wingenbach, Charles E. *The Peace Corps: Who, How and When.* New York: The John Day Co., 1964.

Yoder, John Howard. "France." *Mennonite Encyclopedia* 2, 362.

The Index

The Author

Calvin W. Redekop, Harrisonburg, Virginia, taught at a variety of Mennonite colleges from 1954-1990. He has contributed to diverse denominational organizations and study groups, including Mennonite Economic Development Associates (MEDA) where, maintaining that the Anabaptist witness in economics has long been avoided, he has aimed to foster integration of faith and economic behavior.

Redekop is author of numerous books and publications, including such recent titles as *Leaving Anabaptism: From Evangelical Mennonite Brethren to Fellowship of Evangelical Bible Churches* (Pandora Press U.S., 1998), which draws on Redekop's scholarly insights,combined with the fact that his roots were Evangelical Mennonite Brethren; and *Creation and Environment* (Johns Hopkins, 2000).

Redekop and his wife, Frieda Pellman Redekop, are parents of three adult sons and members of Park View Mennonite Church.